It's who we are
It's what we do

By

Rene Jax

It's who we are
It's what we do

Written
By
Rene Jax

First Printing September 2015

Cover Design
by
Amanda Mullins

Cover photograph
By
Eddie Adams

Photograph used with permission
from
The Associated Press 2015

This book is the work of a diseased mind and is entirely fictional. All characters, people, places, and events portrayed in this book are fictional. Any similarity to reality, or to persons, living or dead is purely coincidental and not intended by the author when she is in or out of her right mind.

DEDICATED

to

Mr. Peter Vacco.

**Whose common sense and wisdom
have guided him through fifteen thousand miles
of North American wilderness**

...and me through the darkness of the human soul

TABLE OF CONTENT

INTRODUCTION

If you've just picked up this book looking for an answer to the eternal question of whether or not humans are intrinsically violent, I will save you the $7.99 for the cost of this book and tell you straight out, YES.

Yes, humans are absolutely and genetically inclined toward violence. It, (violence) is who we are, it is what we do. My entire life I have read one scientist after another proclaim that "Biology is not destiny" They insist that what drives our biology changes which each generation and external influence. They refuse to acknowledge the simple fact that if their statement were true, the world's population would not be exponentially increasing and that violence among humans should have stopped long ago. I counter in this book, that biology is destiny, and to ignore this solitary fact is not only foolish, but also dangerous.

"It" permeates every action, every thought, every instinct, and every reaction to every situation that we encounter in our daily lives. That violence drives our dreams, our inspirations, our lives, our cultures, our wars, our rapes, our music, our population rates, our religions, our paintings, our pollution, and is responsible for the rapid extinction of every other species on Earth. That "IT" will ultimately be responsible for the destruction of the lonely little planet that we inhabit.

"OMFG!" you might say. Yep, that's a hell of a statement isn't it! In this book I lay out the solitary and simple reason for the violence and wars that has plagued human kind since the beginning of time, some two million years ago. Our seemingly inseparable and inalienable right and ability to commit and perpetrate violence upon other species, ourselves and other peoples is built into our DNA and acts to protect us from the world we were born into. This genetic code is at the heart of who we are as individual people, and as a species living amongst others of our own kind, and living with all of the other species of our planet. Scattered about these many pages is the irrefutable evidence that points straight back to our very own DNA as the culprit for all that taints us as a species.

This is not a "Je'accuse". What I have attempted to do in presenting my conclusions to you and wipe away the worthless detritus that has collected around the root cause of human violence. Increasingly there are more and more contemporary writers and philosophers that emphatically state that violence is a learned and cultural manifestation. Their writings are full of lofty justifications and clinical studies that try so very hard, to not come to the conclusion that humans are a violent species. It is almost as if, that by blaming human violence as environmental rather than intrinsic, they can justify further hope in the salvation of our race.

In Alfie Kohn's white paper, "Are humans innately aggressive" he states that, "Clearly, many people — and, in fact, whole cultures — manage quite well without behaving aggressively" and works himself up to a lather trying to persuade himself, and us that "there is no scientific basis for the belief that humans are naturally aggressive and warlike" He is able to rationalize his theory by simply focusing on those rare societies that are the exception, rather than the rule. And while he and many others look deep within society and societal influence on the individual for their reasons to human aggressiveness, they must belittle and dismiss all quantitative conclusions that lead them straight back to my main point and conclusion… humans *are* a violent species. And not just a species that is prone to violence, but a species that has such an evolved sense and capacity for violence that it has put not only our own species in mortal danger, but every living thing on this planet. Our basic and core ability to be violent is risking the extinction of all life on Earth at risk.

Not that I would lose much sleep should our species become completely extinct. We are a most entertaining species.

I believe that as a species we are capable of wondrous and magical things. I know that individually and collectively we have done most amazing things. There are far too many wondrous things that we do, to be listed here. But these are all effects cause based upon by higher-level cooperation and collaboration of our human societies, and do not contradict our violent nature.

As is often repeated to ten-year old children, "Two wrongs do not make a right!" Nor do all of our many right and magical creations made by us, free us from the stench that the violence that we daily perpetrate upon one another creates. Neither does finding clever little mental ways to dance around who we are, move us any closer to finding and implementing real solutions to raining in our natural impulses. Only by all of us accepting ***Who We Are and What We do***, will we be able to move beyond the holocaust that awaits us. I honestly and fully believe that a holocaust is on the near horizon for the human race. Homo sapiens have had a good, if not great run of it on this planet. We, as a species have made it through three massive, long lasting ice ages over the last million years. We have survived through two other minor ones, one as recent as twelve thousand years. Our early ancestors migrated around the entire planet, on foot at a time in our planet's history when there were no seven-eleven's on the planet for them to shop for soda, arrow tips and deer meat. Because of our unique ability to adapt and change, and because of the many tools we learned and continue to learn to produce.

Having just saved you the cost of a Caramel Latte. I suggest you relax in the knowledge that there is absolutely nothing that you and your liberal politics, or Hawk-like propensities can do about murder, rape, shootings, religious wars, or human annihilation. Certainly not anything we as individuals can do to turn any of this around. So just sit back, sip your latte… and watch the fun unfold.

CHAPTER ONE- IT'S WHO WE ARE.

Since the very start of human recorded history, Homo sapiens, our species, have documented the rise of human cultures. In these records, the modern man (both male and female) is still able to see ourselves across time and across the millennia that is human history. There in stone, in parchment, in clay pots, etched in monuments, scribed in papyrus, typed in printed books, and now entered digitally, we can hear the voices of our many ancestors reach out from the past and read the poetry of their lives and societies to us in the present. Their descriptions of violence and wars, is as fresh and relatable to today, as it was when Flavius Josephus wrote "The War on the Jews" in 75 AD.

The very first time that I felt this connection to past lives was when I originally read Plato's Symposium. In it, Plato lays out the Origin of Love. This section of the writing alone is worth the reading of the full text and is as romantic as any current day, Jane Austin or Judith McNaught novel. And though his words are over two thousand years old, coming to me from a different and now dead culture, a different peoples and different language, I was able to completely and utterly related to the emotions, the thoughts and feelings Plato describes for his characters in the text. It is exactly this ability, which allows a person standing in the year 2015 to understand people's emotions and motives of people who lived two or three thousand years ago that is proof positive of the fact that we as an organism have not evolved. It is in this solitary and singular overlooked fact that holds such great and tremendous significance for us in our understanding as a human being, about being a human being.

This is not to say that our family structures and societies have not changed. Nor am I overlooking how our species use and created every complex tool over the last four hundred thousand years. Certainly, how individual nuclear families of Germany lived at the time of Rome's conquest is different from how their ancestors in rural Germany live today.

It is vital that in order to understand who we are, that we don't confuse changes in tools, changes to family structure, society, and global effect with evolution of us as a species. Any sane person who has driven through a Native American Indian reservation immediately sees that the introduction of Eastern American Whites in the early 1800's completely stopped the natural evolution of indigenous American people. I have visited many modern day Navajo, Apache, Paiute, Miwok, and Shoshone Indian reservations of the West and Southwestern United States. Not only have they not fully integrated into Western society after almost two hundred years of interaction, they are intrinsically at odds with much of what white society has heaped upon them. In Canada, nearly fifty percent of its annual budget goes to financial support, benefits, healthcare, fuel, and other additional services for its aboriginal/native Indian/ First Nations and Eskimo populations. Yet, the aboriginal people only accounted for 4.3% of the population. Canada has yet to show any significant improvements in the First Nations family and social structures, or in the poverty level for their $150 billion-dollar yearly investment.

At the time of their conquest, and with no notable exceptions, Native Americans were peoples without any written language. They were at a family and social development level nearly four thousand years behind that of the Western Europeans who came West after 1840. Unlike many of their Central & South American Indian cousins who had developed astronomy and systems of written language and forms of organized government by the mid 1400s, American Indians were still stone-age nomadic peoples. The introduction of a stone age people to nineteenth/twentieth/twenty-first century tools, education and technology has done very little to help evolve the American Indians any more than Western tools have had an impact upon Canada's First Nations Peoples. Even the most warm and fussy liberals who try to paint rosy pictures on how peaceful Native Americans were before white settlers arrived are trying to mislead you.

The viewpoint that Native Americans were saints is rebuked by noted historian John Hogan

He writes:

"Native Americans definitely waged war (sic... on other tribes) long before Europeans showed up. The evidence is especially strong in the American Southwest, where archaeologists have found numerous skeletons (dated before whites arrived in the New World) with projectile points embedded in them and other marks of violence; war seems to have surged during periods of drought."

This proves evolution of a people's tools, or the introduction of an advanced society with the Stone Age peoples, is not the same thing as the evolution of a human being at its family structure level. And it certainly does nothing to change the fundamental traits of the organism itself.

With this in mind, it is very important that we take a step back to appreciate the fact that just as Native Americans have not changed after being subjected to Western European societal influences for the last six-hundred years, that the core of who you and I has not changed as a result of those very same influences over the last one hundred thousand years. Our tools have changed and evolved, our families and family structures have changed, our societies have changed, ***but who we are has not.***

Coming back to our original question of what is the core reason that makes humans such a violent and aggressive species? It is so simple a thing that all researchers on the subject of violence and aggression overlook it, downplay it, or don't give it any thought at all. It is the most basic drive for all species, for all viruses, for all fish, and for all mammals.

It is the need for the organism to survive!

This most basic drive for any organism to survive. Survive by procreating; by replicating, by infecting; by shooting sperm over eggs, by what every means we have evolved, in order to produce another copy, another being, another sequence of virus, and another life form.

Procreation of species is The Prime Directive (TPD) for our species.

The Prime Directive colors and taints all other endeavors and drives of the human species. It affects how we come together as families and how families build upon societies. Everything we have done, everything we have created and everything we have built as societies is built around the need for us as an organism to survive. Every rape, every murder, every assault, every war and global conflict there has ever been are outcomes from TPD upon our psychic.

Forget individuality. Forget what your church or parents taught you about your place in the Universe. Forget about Freud, Jung, Masters & Johnson, Jesus, Mohammed and Moses. Forget about Carl Sagen, Steven Hawking, NASA and their probe to Pluto. Forget Plato, Socrates, Marcus Aurelius and Shakespeare. Forget about Abe Lincoln, Hitler, Stalin, and Genghis Khan.

Stop for Pete's sake; PLEASE stop taking yourself so bloody seriously.

You are not your:
- JOB
- CAR YOU DRIVE
- HOUSE YOU OWN
- NEIGHBORHOOD YOU LIVE IN
- INCOME (HIGH OR LOW)
- AMOUNT OF MONEY IN BANK

- o THE POSITION YOU HOLD IN A
  GOVERNMENT
- o JEWELRY YOU WEAR
- o WHAT COLLEGE YOU ATTENDED

You are nothing more (or less) than a living organism that walks. The Prime Directive that is in every DNA fibre in your body propels you toward ***one and only one goal***. That goal is to survive by replicating.

Some women reading this may be sitting there thinking, "Well yes, I can sort of see her point. But really, I am my own person, a modern woman. I am almost forty years old and never had the need to have a child. I am not bound by these primitive urges." I get it! A lot of my friends over the years say they have *chosen* not to have children. Their relationship with their partner is not solid, their finances aren't good, their careers are just taking off, on and on and on. They're all excuses. You want to know why I know they are excuses? Because they are all built around rationalizations for NOT HAVING A CHILD. Having a child is the norm because it is The Prime Directive of our organism. The need to replicate ourselves is all that we are supposed to do as an organism. Not sail around the world, not build cities, not create computers, and not design fashion. Everything we do other than follow The Prime Directive is accidental and unnecessary. I've been to Vatican City several times and as magnificent and glorious as it is, it is just more fluff. The only thing that should matter to us, to you, to family, and to society is The Prime Directive.

But as we all know, The Prime Directive isn't everything to us, is it?

I started writing this book over four years ago. It started out with a very simple premise. That early premise was that the prime reason for all of humanities aliments was from our selfishness. Regardless of what else we as a people did, we always fell back upon our intrinsic selfishness. I wasn't really condemning people for it, just making note of it. I've always believed that you can't change a sow's ear into a silk purse. But then about a year ago, I was watching a TV special on Ebola viruses and the speaker mentioned that viruses only want to find ways to infect more people, so they, the virus can continue growing and living. And in that moment I knew. Everything I've read and learned about humans and human society over the last fifty years made sense. Every war, conflict, every murder made some sort of simple, easy to understand sense. It was right there in front of me and now it made sense. Countless other, smarter and more brilliant thinkers and philosophers than I, really smart people over thousands of years have looked right at it and ignored it, or discounted The Prime Directive's impact upon them and human society. Homo Sapiens advancements in family and societal structures, or clever use of tools, our unique ability to change and modify our living environments, have all overshadowed our very humble roots. But all of these amazing changes to the more advance aspects of our lives have not changed who we are _at our core_.

The Prime Directive mandates that we survive at all costs. Since we are not immortal, we must replicate, we must replicate, we must replicate, we must replicate, we must replicate, we must replicate, we must replicate, we must replicate, we must replicate, we must replicate, we must replicate, we must replicate, we must replicate, we must replicate, we must replicate.

CHAPTER TWO - LONGEVITY

Mating with the opposite sex does that replication. The act of replication is not enough to satisfy The Prime Directive. Once the female egg is fertilized, then for the next nine months, both the female and the fetus must eat. They must have shelter, they must be safe from harm, and they must not exert themselves. Once the female gives birth, the child must then be taken care of for nearly 12 years before it is a self-sufficient life form and can strike out on its own. It is from this very long growth period that human family structure is derived and developed. If you look at other animal's gestation periods, life spans and their subsequent family structures, you can start to see why their family structures are so vastly different from humans.

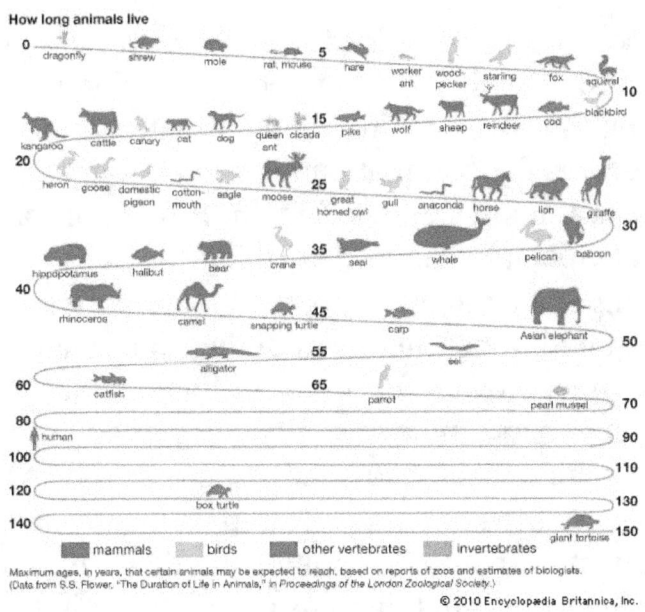

Maximum ages, in years, that certain animals may be expected to reach, based on reports of zoos and estimates of biologists. (Data from S.S. Flower, "The Duration of Life in Animals," in Proceedings of the London Zoological Society.)

© 2010 Encyclopædia Britannica, Inc.

Out human family structure must support an off spring for over a decade in order for it not to be eaten by a predator. If you think our contemporary world is a dangerous place now, and it's hard to raise your daughter to the age of eighteen; imagine back a million years ago. You and your tribe were nomadic, and were forced to follow the food supply. Even in the moist and lush Savanna that existed in East Africa at the time, a square mile of land could barely support two humans. More humans needed more food, and had to travel more mileage to find it. That need to feed, dominated the movement of every tribe. The larger the number of tribe members, the greater the need to feed, and on and on and on. Think back to all of your ancient history. If the land people lived on could support the early tribes, why do you think our early ancestors would leave East Africa and travel to Phoenix on foot?

Another factor that helped to get our ancestors focus off of their need to replicate and to begin creating tools, developing family structures, and ultimately social structures. It is the fact that humans lived longer than any of the other animals in the kingdom. It was our longer life span that helped to change everything for us as a species.

The longer an animal's life, the longer period of interaction with other members of the tribe. That longer period of time allowed for more conflicts within the tribe between members, and eventually rules of how tribe members were expected to behave came into being.

The longer life span also allowed us more opportunities at reproducing off spring. Looking at other animals, they produce dozens, if not hundreds of off spring in the hopes that a few will survive to keep their species alive. With shorter life spans, more competition for food, greater chances of being killed as food, they must literally give as many of their species a chance of life to increase the probability of success of their species. It is a numbers game on a grand and deadly scale. Human beings on the other hand had a few tactical advantages that other species didn't. Out slightly larger brain allowed us to store more historical data, which in turn gave us a tactical advantage evaluating risks, dangers, consequences of actions that many of our animal competition did not. Planned action, and the ability (using lessons learned and logic) to quickly respond to changes in the situation will beat out a simple reflexive response to stimuli every single time.

Coming back to my original premise, I think it is also wise to point out the fact that the concept of love does not come into the replication equation for any virus, plant or animal species. Including for human beings. I will go into this deeper in a later chapter, but I bring it up here as a cautionary note. What humans call love is nothing more than a hormonal response to the organism's need to survive. Without the body's releasing a chemical driver for both sexes to procreate, our species would have died off at the very beginning. Without that driver, I just cannot imagine a primitive homo sapien male and female both figuring out the mechanics of sexual intercourse. Stranger things have happened, but if these chemical drivers where not intrinsic to who we are, were they not natural and completely overpowering to both sexes, then we as a species would never existing.

These chemical drivers, which we now generally call love or personal attraction is the key reason, we as a species keep on going. It is the grease that lubricates the wheels of our existence on this planet. We must never confuse the tools we can make, or the family and societal structures that come out of this foundation with the biological need the organism has for survival.

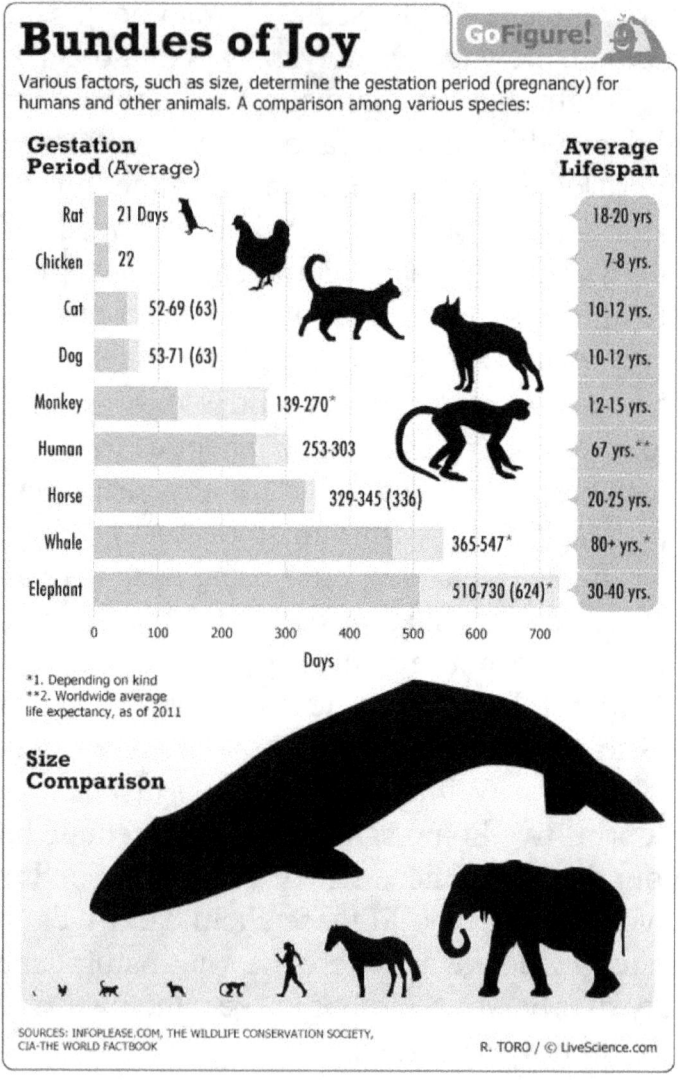

Bundles of Joy

Go Figure!

Various factors, such as size, determine the gestation period (pregnancy) for humans and other animals. A comparison among various species:

Gestation Period (Average)		Average Lifespan
Rat	21 Days	18-20 yrs
Chicken	22	7-8 yrs.
Cat	52-69 (63)	10-12 yrs.
Dog	53-71 (63)	10-12 yrs.
Monkey	139-270*	12-15 yrs.
Human	253-303	67 yrs.**
Horse	329-345 (336)	20-25 yrs.
Whale	365-547*	80+ yrs.*
Elephant	510-730 (624)*	30-40 yrs.

0   100   200   300   400   500   600   700

Days

*1. Depending on kind
**2. Worldwide average life expectancy, as of 2011

Size Comparison

SOURCES: INFOPLEASE.COM, THE WILDLIFE CONSERVATION SOCIETY, CIA-THE WORLD FACTBOOK

R. TORO / © LiveScience.com

CHAPTER THREE - VIOLENCE

In Chapter Two we looked at the basic foundation of our organism. No surprise to any of you. Everything I mentioned was in keeping with science's current technical understanding of how things have shaped up. I believe that the fruits and folly of what our species has created upon the surface of our organism's Prime Directive have blinded researchers. Nearly all scholarly studies spell out everything I just wrote, but then quickly runs away from focusing on The Prime Directive, to recount in painstakingly dry terms the history and types of tools early man created. After which, they rush off further onto the role that families played and how societies were built up over the last sixty thousand years or so. All that I can figure out from observing this fast sprint away from a detailed examination of our primordial beginnings is that the writer believes it is either too boring, too simple, or too elementary to hold their readers to the page for more than 500 words. It is in their quest to scurry away that they fail to connect all of the dots of our human world. Our lives are not made up of just stone cutting tools, human collaboration during hunting, the rise of agriculture societies, or the development of electronic tools and machines. In the 1980s I fell in love with A Bronowski's The Accent of Man series. For the first time in one place, he showed a history of the fascinating occurrences that helped make up part of the landscape of human development.

I write this not to extol unrecognized virtues on our organism that others have failed to address, but to recalibrate humanity's expectations for our life form. Without a reset of expectations for human kind, (both male and female), without seeing the one true reason for all of the violence we are capable of, we can never hope to move beyond our primal - intrinsic instincts for self-protection. We must move beyond our self-preoccupation, beyond our self-propagation and beyond our selfishness with every other species on this dear planet.

All of this starts with an acceptance of The Prime Directive as our sole driving force. To us, as an organism… surviving is all that matters. Survival for the sake of our off spring is the only reason the childbearing adults live after giving birth. Unlike many other species that die off after the mating ritual, humans must continue providing for their children for over a decade.

As any contemporary parent will painfully acknowledge, supporting their children never seems to end, and twenty first century birth is more like serving a life sentence at Alcatraz prison. The need to protect our offspring from threats is also built into our organism's DNA. The Prime Directive mandates the ability for human males to quickly respond to external threats, to become violent. The two go hand in hand. Survival of our species and the ability to quickly become violent to defend our children, our females, our homes, our food supplies, and our families is critical survival. It is from our long life spans that this secondary reflex becomes so ingrained into our upper level relationships.

It can, and should be questioned whether or not this reflex is not just designed and implemented during childbearing periods. I wish it were so. But five thousand years of written human history shows us that human violence by males cannot be turned off. Studies show that as human males live longer, that the percentage of perpetrators of violence decreases dramatically. Males of advanced age do not stop being violent however, any more than our females are able to walk away from, or can turn off their natural mating or maternal instincts. While not all human females wish to have children, nearly 99.99% have a driven need to mate.

Violence in defense of family is a given and major part of The Prime Directive. To this very day, the majority of human laws support and codify the killing of others who threaten the family. Few crimes are thought of as callous as that of assault and injury of a child. The killer of a mother/with child will almost always receive a death sentence. This DNA need to protect the survivability of our organism is clearly seen played out on the evening news in the year 2015. Yet while remnants of The Prime Directive fill countless volumes of our legal system the appreciation and respect for TPD is held hostage to modern conventions and mistaken beliefs about who we are and what we do. Violence in contemporary society is seen as unnecessary and outdated. It is nearly always seen as the exception, not the rule. Humans are now viewed in the context of a "civilized society" and ruled by laws based on a perception of our roles in a civilized setting. The imperative word is "Civilized" People's perception of themselves is that of the upper tier of social level functioning, while totally ignoring the facts, the reality of who we are and what we do.

Again, don't confuse our tools, our family structure, and our societal structures with who we are. We are an organism that is by design, built to breed and are violent at a moment's notice.

I just went online and found the Oxford Dictionary definition of violence.

Definition of violence in English:
Noun

1. Behavior involving physical force intended to <u>hurt</u>, damage, or kill someone or something.

1.1 Strength of emotion or an unpleasant or <u>destructive</u> natural force:

1.2 Law The <u>unlawful</u> exercise of physical force or <u>intimidation</u> by the <u>exhibition</u> of such force.

I find 1.1 very telling. "A destructive natural force." And yet, neither this dictionary, nor any of the countless other dictionary definitions for the word will take ownership of the word as a basic trait of our human organism. Somewhere, on one line of a dictionary it should read:

Violence:Grammar, Noun

1.0: A biologically produced reaction in the human organism to threats or danger.

1.1: A reaction to real or perceived threats or challenges to the organism intended to challenge the threatening person or condition, to frighten off, to defend the organism, or attack said person or condition in order for the threatened organism, its mate(s) and or its offspring to live and survive.

1.2: The act of physical force necessary for the organism to survive a threat.

Seeing how common day society has so radically disassociated itself from The Prime Directive, it makes perfect sense that we now live in violence torn societies that seem incapable of dealing effectively with the outer social manifestations of our basic human organism DNA. In many articles written by social scientists, they loudly proclaim (and there is a social acceptance of their beliefs) that violence is the outcome and out cropping due to poverty, illiteracy, racial prejudice, discrimination, bad parenting, religious beliefs, the tools used to commit the crime of violence.

Recently in the US state of Tennessee, a Muslim named Mohammad Abdlezeez went on a killing spree. In the wake of his actions, five United States service men lay dead. Though he left no message explaining his actions, there was an immediate call by liberals to round up and confiscate all of the guns in the country. This happens time and time around the globe. Ignorant people focus on the Tier Two level tools used by humans, rather than associate the specific act, with the specific organism. Mohammad Abudlezeez and every other mass killer we read about are simply acting out physically to a real or perceived threat. The tools these men use are irrelevant to the equation.

For humans, violence serves the organism. If we look to nature, we see many other creative means that species have learned to adapt to survival threats. Everything from porcupines to blowfish and squids has capabilities designed specifically to helping that species survive and have offspring.

It is our unusually long life span that warrants the ongoing and continued violent reaction to threats. Many species just lay their eggs and leave the area, saying to their fertilized eggs as they go, "Goodbye, good luck, don't let the birds eat you!" With these species, The Prime Directive is to flee, rather than to fight. They have neither the DNA capability to deal violently with other animal competitors, nor the physical design to carry out such a response. Humans on the other hand are built very well for it. Our males have strong arms and legs, stamina, and bones and muscles covering major organs. We excel at being able to respond violently, because that what we are designed to do.

There are those kind readers who would like me to point out that our species has over the last two million years of evolution created seven-elevens and hired police to protect us. We have written laws and instituted courts to ensure those laws are followed. We have mutually agreed to live together in large cities without the need or use of violence. They would very much like for me to tell you that we are not living in the jungle any longer. There is no need to be violent ever again. As Mr. Kohn points out, not ever modern day society in our world has a propensity toward violence. This is proof positive to him that mankind is not a violent species and that other conditions are at fault for human violence. If only correlation was causation. As defined in the following chart:

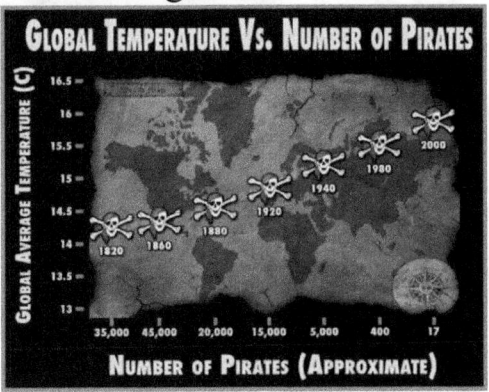

Here we can see that the decrease in the number of Pirates since the 1500's correlates to the increase in global average temperature. Just as Mr. Kohn's pointing out that there are societies that report little violence amongst the population proves that humans are not a violent species. And I do agree with him in a sick kind of way. I don't really think we are violent. Few normal, sane people get up with the thoughts of who are they going to kill today. But our species has a built in trigger that predominates all other higher brain functioning.

We do however get up every day as an organism with The Prime Directive ***STILL*** driving our decisions. SURVIVE, MATE, PROCREATE, SURVIVE, FIND FOOD, SURVIVE, SURVIVE, *SURVIVE*!

In order to better understand where The Prime Directive has gone astray, we need to take a closer look at the more advanced levels of human life.

CHAPTER FOUR – THE FOUR TIERS

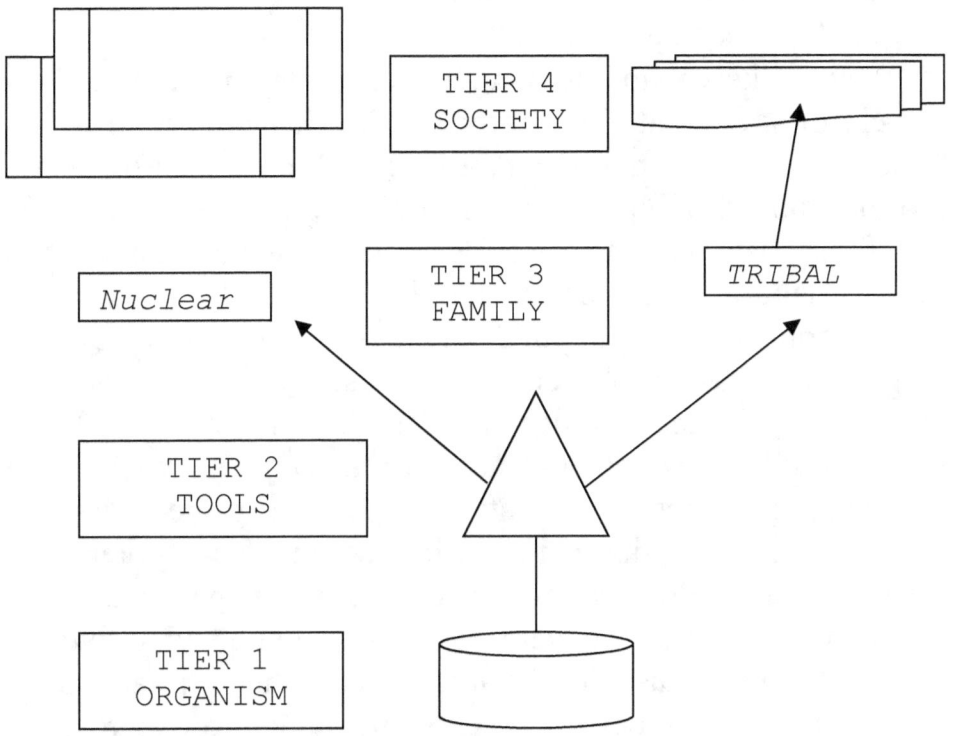

To help explain the world in which we find ourselves, I have broken down the progression of human development that has taken place over the last two million years. As previously and laboriously (yet elegantly) stated in the previous chapters, the foundation level of our lives on this planet is Tier One – The Organism. It is the foundation by which we experience and express ourselves as an animal. It is the subsequent levels, Tier's two through four that I now concern this lecture. It is in these Tiers that human life expresses itself.

Tier Two is that of the tools we find or produce that allow our organism to survive and fulfill The Prime Directive. As we all know from having seen the movie, *2001 A Space Odyssey*, our ancestors most likely used an animal bone as our first tools.

More likely than not, humans quickly learned to use rocks or sticks that allowed them to kill fish and small game. As time went on and our need for more specific uses of our tools developed, more specific tools developed. To this very day, humans use tools to cut stone and animal flesh that are almost identical to those that early humanoids in the Ethiopia Savanna over a million years ago. These basic tools need not necessarily change over the millennia since the use of the tool has not change. The knife I use to clean the guts and skin off a quail I've killed is doing the exact movements on exactly the same type of game bird or varmint that a cutting tool in used in outer China of 100,000 years ago. Tools allow our species to live in a world that we were not very well evolved to live in. Cutting tools used to cut and process other animals pelts, allow our species to live in colder and more extreme climates than our bodies could ever hope to adapt to.

Were it not for the discovery and production of fire, our ancestors might certainly have died out during any of the previous major ice ages. The wheel as a tool is little changed in today's usage versus when it was first created over five thousand years ago. Firearms are a recent development in around 1300. In the seven centuries hence, firearms still utilize not only the same principles, but also many of the same chemicals as the original fire sticks and cannons that were created. The metal casing we call a bullet is now over one hundred and fifty years old and showing few signs of disappearance or even modification from its original design. This is because the *use* of these weapons is the same as it was seven hundred years ago. The simple chemistry that allows for the rapid expansion of gas from the gun powder, which then pushes the projectile out of the barrel and onto a target still provides the same effect for today's hunter and or killer as it did in ancient Europe or China.

Anthropologists and sociologists continue to confuse the development of our tools with the development of us as a species. Once again, correlation is not causation. (I just love the pirate chart!) The Prime Directive mandates our survival instinct and we move heaven and earth to find a means, a path, a tool, or a process to meet that internally driven expectation. Tools allow our limited, poorly evolved and equipped species to fulfill The Prime Directive.

The tool never changes our basic organism. The Prime Directive is never changed by the tool.

The tools we create and use do however effect change to the other Tiers. The tools we use can and do change the family structure. Washing machines and electric refrigerators changed the amount of free time females had in modern times. That additional free time allowed her to spend more time performing other family and societal duties. The tools we use do change the society structure. The creation of the first airplane by the Wright Brothers have allowed the greatest cross cultural interchange in the shortest time in our specie's history.

There is the argument that our tools created more sanitary conditions, better health and nutrition in our societies and hence, produced longer life spans for our species. But this is only part of the equation. Our tools, family and societal structures only act to serve TPD. Longer life spans do not change The Prime Directive.

I think with the sole exception of birth control as a tool, all else should serve TPD. Even birth control does not stop the drive to mate and procreate, only the ability to produce off spring. Speaking from experience, birth control allowed me far greater practice to mate than I would have had without it.

Tier Three is that of family structure.

A unified family structure began to develop most probably due to the gradual increase in tribal populations grew. When our ancestors where simply another animal amongst hundreds of other animals in the Savanna, every other animal, including humans were a threat to survival. Without the ability to run down to 7-11 for a hot dog and coke, our Tier One Prime Directive would have ensured that all other competitors for the limited food supply then available in that region would be thought of as direct threats. I suspect that due to a scarcity of food, it would have taken generations before our ancestors befriended others of our species in any large numbers. And most small family units would have lived a life not unlike most other animals of the day. It is within the Tier Three family structure that how male and female relate to one another are were played out beyond the physical requirements and influences of the Tier One Organism.

It is at this level that individual organisms (people) slowly began to define themselves as individuals and in relationship to the family structure began developing. Family (and I almost don't like to use the word due to so many common connotations associated with the word) is the first relationship our individual organism has with other organisms outside the placenta. The *in utero* experience on the fetus though important, is not really a social relationship. Once born the interactions of the various family members have a striking effect on the organism's social development and functioning. This relationship has repeatedly been examined and commented on for the last three thousand years. All sorts of theories have been put forth about the impact family upbringing has upon the individual and their later, adult behavior. But no writer or philosopher has ever wished to tie the adult human behavior directly back to the organism level, until now. I contend that our philosophies about human development have had a blind spot, a unintentional weakness in them due to the exclusion of any mention or addition of The Prime Directive in the equation of why we do what we do on a family and social level.

Let's talk a moment about a very uncomfortable and disquieting subject, that of Pedophilia. Currently defined as: a psychiatric disorder where an individual over the age of 16 has a deep-rooted desire to have sexual relationships with children. I have read dozens of case studies about this and no one "knows" what causes it. The list of possible culprits goes on and on in the medical literature. It's very simple and I hate to suggest it, but… The Prime Directive.

The Prime Directive mandates that our males find suitable mates to procreate. Just as it has been repeatedly proven that female animals in the herd are looking the Alpha male who is the best to breed with, (for a variety of reasons) so it is with males. They want young, healthy and stout females that can live through the pregnancy, and live long enough to help nurture the offspring.

The imperative words here are: YOUNG AND HEALTHY.

Not middle-aged and works out twice a week. Or in her twenties, smokes and does drugs. And certainly not in her forties and has worked in an office for fifteen years, but wants to have children before the clock stops ticking. Young, healthy and able to hold up for the marathon that is child rearing.

Going back to Plato's Symposium on the Origins of Love is a very telling description of a pedophilia love:

"They were being destroyed, when Zeus in pity of them invented a new plan: he turned the parts of generation round to the front, for this had not been always their position and they sowed the seed no longer as hitherto like grasshoppers in the ground, but in one another; and after the transposition the male generated in the female in order that by the mutual embraces of man and woman they might breed, and the race might continue; or if man came to man they might be satisfied, and rest, and go their ways to the business of life: so ancient is the desire of one another which is implanted in us, reuniting our original nature, making one of two, and healing the state of man.

Each of us when separated, having one side only, like a flat fish, is but the indenture of a man, and he is always looking for his other half. Men who are a section of that double nature which was once called Androgynous are lovers of women; adulterers are generally of this breed, and also adulterous women who lust after men: the women who are a section of the woman do not care for men, but have female attachments; the female companions are of this sort. **But they who are a section of the male follow the male, and while they are young, being slices of the original man, they hang about men and embrace them,** *and they are themselves the best of boys and youths, because they have the most manly nature. Some indeed assert that they are shameless, but this is not true; for they do not act thus from any want of shame, but because they are valiant and manly, and have a manly countenance, and they embrace that which is like them.* **And these when they grow up become our statesmen, and these only, which is a great proof of the truth of what I am saying. When they reach manhood they are loves of youth,** *and are not naturally inclined to marry or beget children,-if at all, they do so only in obedience to the law; but they are satisfied if they may be allowed to live with one another unwedded; and such a nature is prone to love and ready to return love, always embracing that which is akin to him. And when one of them meets with his other half, the* *actual half of himself, whether he be a lover of youth or a lover of another sort, the pair are lost in an amazement of love and friendship and intimacy, and would not be out of the other's sight, as I may say, even for a moment: these are the people who pass their whole lives together;* **yet they could not explain what they desire of one another. For the intense yearning which each of them has towards the other does not appear to be the desire of lover's intercourse, but of something else which the soul of either evidently desires and cannot tell, and of which she has only a dark and doubtful presentiment***.*

Suppose Hephaestus, with his instruments, to come to the pair who are lying side, by side and to say to them, "What do you people want of one another?" they would be unable to explain. And suppose further, that when he saw their perplexity he said: "Do you desire to be wholly one; always day and night to be in one another's company? for if this is what you desire, I am ready to melt you into one and let you grow together, so that being two you shall become one, and while you live a common life as if you were a single man, and after your death in the world below still be one departed soul instead of two-I ask whether this is what you lovingly desire, and whether you are satisfied to attain this?"-there is not a man of them who when he heard the proposal would deny or would not acknowledge that this meeting and melting into one another, this becoming one instead of two, was the very expression of his ancient need. And the reason is that human nature was originally one and we were a whole, and the desire and pursuit of the whole is called love. There was a time, I say, when we were one, but now because of the wickedness of mankind God has dispersed us, as the Arcadians were dispersed into villages by the Lacedaemonians. And if we are not obedient to the gods, there is a danger that we shall be split up again and go about in basso-relievo, like the profile figures having only half a nose which are sculptured on monuments, and that we shall be like tallies."

"but of something else which the soul of either evidently desires and cannot tell"

Plato is reaching out over two thousand years to tell us that there is something driving adults to have sex with young people. Over these many centuries since, we have outlawed the practice, blasphemed it, punished it, imprisoned it, and criminalized it. And some people still desire to have sex with young people. This primal drive is a permanent fixture in our species' DNA. Look around the city you live in. How many billboards and magazine covers do you see that extol the sexuality of women in their fifties? They don't! and the reason they don't is that **all of contemporary marketing is geared toward** child bearing age adults.

This cold, hard fact is such a truism that I don't have to submit any type of my own research to justify the statement. It is a fact. Even today, with all of the hype around living longer and better, eating better and exercising and being more vibrant in old age. It all means nothing to the organism. It is irrelevant fluff that does not serve The Prime Directive.

I believe the degree by which individuals act upon their natural sexual attraction to young (less than 16yrs of age) is determined by Tier Three and Four influences. These lovers of youth all demonstrate and have a need for power over their lovers. They need to dominate and control that which they idolize sexually. They see in the youth, perfection and grace that they themselves lack.

In Japan, the desire is not hidden away deep with closets or basements, but is out in the open throughout the country. Lolita Fashion, based on the film Lolita with James Mason, permeates fashion and dress among Japanese women, young and old. It is not uncommon while walking in the Roppongi Hills section of Japan to see middle-aged women dressed up as young schools girls. This is played out in nearly every Anime comic book and movie.

Strange? Sick? Demented? Not if you look at this as a Tier One basic requirement seeping out of our ancestral past and into contemporary family and social dynamics. (I just don't think any Ethiopian ancestor has ever owned a dress like that looked like this,) but yet the appeal of a young (healthy) person to breed with has been, and is still in each of us.

With this in mind, we can now see how personalities and environmental conditions within the family structure quickly begin to affect the individual organism's Prime Directive. And again, we see how our longer life spans allow for more prolonged influences to adversely affect the person. While initially our Tier Three biological family unit was driven by TPD to cradle, nurture and protect us, the longer we live in this unit, the more ancillary issues our species has to contend with that are not directly related to The Prime Directive. The old saying, "When you're up to your ass in alligators, it's hard to remember your initial goal was to drain the swamp." Immediately comes to mind.

What once, long – long ago was a built-in need to ensure our species' survivability, has now become, well… FAMILY. And we all know what comes with that! Spending holidays with Grandma, and birthdays, and parents trying to control teenagers. It is economics, and allowances, and doing laundry. It's cleaning rooms, and going to school and crashing the car and premature sex with boyfriends. Family is everything that our species, when it first stood upright some two million years ago for the very first time, *never* saw coming. I bet that if our ancestors would have been told what they were about to start, they would have went back on all fours and ran away from their mates.

But it's too late now to change any of this.

What we can do is understand Who We Are and What We Do. And appreciate where we are coming from and how to this day, it still affects our lives and the decisions we make.

You will also notice on the chart that I have differentiated between two types of common family structures.

Type One is a Nuclear family structure. This family consists solely of the immediate members of the male and or female and their offspring. These family structures are seen mostly in Europe from around 12000 years ago. Many burial sites that have been uncovered have found related family members together, and rarely any unrelated persons. During recorded history of the region, the Nuclear family structure has been *the predominate structure* for the last two thousand years. Though there are variances of this structure depending between Northern and Southern Europe, the foundation for the Nuclear family structure remains constant.

Type Two Family structure is a Tribal, or nomadic family structure. This family consists not only of the immediate members of the male and female and their offspring, but also siblings of the male and female, parents from both sides of the primary adults, as well first and second cousins. These families stay together to the joint interests and benefit to all family members. They also benefit from larger numbers of family participants to throw into any conflict with other tribes who are in direct competition or threat to.

We must differentiate between the two family structures, since each respective structure developed different norms, laws, customs and behaviors. These family structures sit above the Tier Two tools, and exert tremendous influences on how tools are developed and used differently between them, based on needs of that particular structure. The differences between the two family structures will ultimately affect how TPD is played out by individuals.

Since Nuclear family structures are small by design, the individuals in that structure must learn to quickly collaborate with external families for food, housing, and to combat threats with other hostile Nuclear families in order to survive. Nomadic families on the other hand, are more self-supporting due to the larger numbers that exist within the tribe. They have much less need for exchanges with external tribes, and as a result, collaboration as a tool is rarely used. Historically when tribal, Nomadic peoples come together to trade in villages and towns (Tier Four societies), rivalries conflicts naturally erupted. These because very problematic, since there was no commonality between two different tribes taboos and mores due to Nomadic tribes historically being more suspicious and threatened by the other Nomadic tribes. To this day, the act of bartering for goods and services in Africa and the Middle East is nothing less than a blood sport. With the individual seller of items always trying to keep the upper hand in the transaction.

As I mentioned earlier, it is in Tier Three structures that our species experience life as something other than an organism. After years of studying biological organisms, I find it most amazing that the human species organism has the ability to build social networks that are truly external to themselves. Perhaps we don't have the mind to understand the Armillaria ostoyae, popularly known as the honey mushroom. It is the largest organism in the world and covers over two thousand acres in Eastern Oregon. Whither it is our lack of capacity to understand it, or that we have not yet made a tool to communicate with it. But compared to this mushroom, alone in a remote forest, human capacity to build families and societies is to be much admired.

Had providence decided to limit the human species gestation period, time to adult hood, or life span, our family and social structures would have turned out completely differently. We are now seeing radical changes to our family and social structures due to an increase in our life spans. At the start of the 1800's, the average human lifespan was only 40 years. And by 1900 it had risen to 45. But over the past one hundred years it has doubled. (in 1st and 2nd world countries) Though there were a number of key conditions within the family and society structures that changed in order for this trend to develop, these changes quickly came back into the structures and precipitated further changes among the groups. These constant changes are cyclical and generate more and more changes with each passing. But what they don't change. What they can't possibly change is The Prime Directive of the organism.

If you imagine building a house in the country, the first thing you do is draw out a design and after clearing the land; you pour a concrete foundation the size and shape of the ultimate structure. Within that concrete you will place pipes for water and sewer drainage. You will also account for the load upon the foundation from the upper floors. That area of foundation for the patio will naturally have need for less concrete since there are no load bearing walls and stories above it. It is upon this concrete that the walls, floors, ceilings, and additional stories are built. Once constructed, changes in the nature of the use of a particular room, or color of walls, and even the removal of a bathroom in the second floor master bedroom does not change the foundation.

If in your skepticism of my argument you bring up the human appendix. The appendix was thought to be used for digesting leaves when we were part of the primate's family. It may be a vestigial organ of ancient humans that has degraded to nearly nothing over the course of evolution. The very long cecum of some herbivorous animals, such as found in the horse or the koala, seems related to human appendix and does appear to support this kind of theory.

But this is pure speculation. There are other theories that suggest it is still used to this day as an organ dealing with our immunization against viruses. Nobody really knows, and to suggest that our bodies have evolved through evolution, rather than simple nutrition is unsubstantiated. And it will never be substantiated due to the fact that there are hundreds of thousands of years of human history that we will forever be blind and ignorant to. Our species has only been recording the outside temperature for under a hundred years, and only in a few cities. The study of volcanoes as a science is less than a a hundred years old. Surgery as a medical science has only been around since the start of World War Two. Surgery as a carpenter and butcher has been around for a couple of thousand years. Surgery during the American Civil War was closer to a butcher's meet shop than to the medical science that it pretends to be today. I had to have my gallbladder removed about six months ago. Right there in black and white on my authorization for surgery it clearly stated the following: *I understand that the practice of medicine and surgery is not an exact science and that diagnosis and treatment may involve risks of injury or even death. I acknowledge that no guarantees have been made to me regarding the result of examination or treatment in the hospital.*

Truly, the concrete foundation is like the DNA of our organism. The room layout is our Tier Three family structures; the use of those rooms is our Tier Four societal structures, and plumbing, electrical, doors, windows, kitchen, fireplace and air-conditioning our Tier Two tools.

Tier Four represents the highest level of human relations, that of society. Societies are the accumulation of multiple smaller, Tier Three family structures.. Tier Four societies continue the development and codification of rules, laws, taboos, and social roles which are based upon the family rules of law. They are most usually marked by the rigidity and adherence to relatively well-defined social normalization of roles for the individual organism. This is due to a society having multiple kinds and types of families congregating together in large numbers, and the resulting need for social order. Lake of social order within large populations negates any kind of positive benefits from the congregation of peoples into that society. Where as Tier Four societies are predominated by the need for commerce, they began to gather together based on religious, language, sexual orientation, and ethnic commonalities. Upper Tier human societies are the by-product of homo sapien over-population rather than a natural, well-organized response to Tier Three family needs.

As Tier Four societies grow in size, they create and demand far more natural resources than had the Tier Three families continued to live remotely and separately. The coming together of families requires far greater physical infrastructure and service demands. And the benefits from this conglomeration of families exact a hefty price from the families in terms of service and or taxes to support the society. The Tier One organism eventually lives to be of service to the Tier Four society, rather than it serving the individual.

Nothing in the above equation changes The Prime Directive.

What does change is how the TPD is made manifest within the family and within the society. What changes is that the individual is no longer protected and nurtured by the family. What changes is that the individual is let adrift to find appropriate mates to satisfy the prime directive. What changes is the fact that the family is no longer the arbiter on what behavior is or is not appropriate for individual family members. What changes is that abhorrent behavior on the part of individuals is not longer quickly identified and dealt with inside the family. What changes is the individual now lives in a constant state of threat due to the uncertainty of their status within the greater society. What changes is that many individuals now relinquish control for their own health, safety, and security to the state, which because it is a social collective rather than a individual family is not set up, and never will be set up to deal with individual members of society…individually.

And along with the extreme financial demands all of this requires to maintain, society is forced to demand continual respect / worship from every individual, regardless of any personal or familial moral beliefs or practices that are contrary to societies. When the society places such a heavy burden on the individuals in the family, it (the family) loses all its ability to raise, support, nurture, protect and educate the individual organism.

It is not a coincidence that when societies demand conformity to such a far reaching extent that they are called "Nanny States"

In a landmark US Supreme Court ruling, the court decided 5-4 in favor of mandating to all the 50 US States that marriage between homosexuals was legal. This, despite the fact that near 20 of those states had voter-sponsored legislation that ruled it wasn't. This is a remarkable development in the history of world societies! Here you have five, un-elected lawyers determining public policy and social norms for 330 million people. Even though there are only about 1 million gays and lesbians in the country. That's 1/3 of 1 percent of the population dictating what is socially acceptable to the remaining 99.66% of the country's population. This shows just how far modern day societies structures have moved from their original purpose.

Due to the ever-increasing Tier Four demands for taxes, for social order, for bodies to fight their wars, for allegiance and for control of the individual, the rulers of societies have usurped the responsibility of the family alpha male and family structure altogether. Common sense for the sake of the organism's survivability is no longer required for the individual. Rather than individual thought and responsibility being an outcropping of the natural order, those organism traits have been supplanted by the needs of society. Society Structures have now become the organism's family, rather than simply a response to the recent exponential population growth, and need for collaboration of families drawn together for shared benefit.

CHAPTER FIVE -A BROKEN WORLD

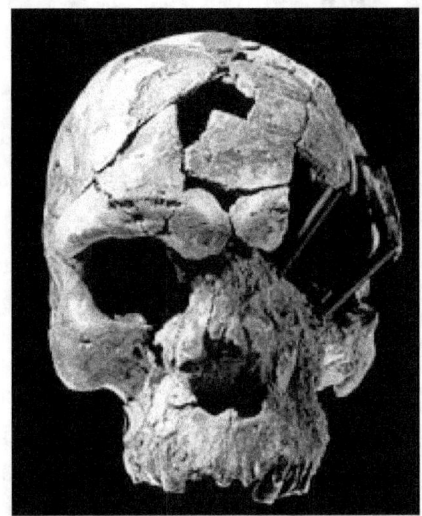

above: Herto Erectus 160,000 yrs old

In this and following chapters I will go into specific social and family issues that have resulted from those structures losing connection or an understanding of our Tier One self. This original self still exists. We as that organism who first walked upright over a million years ago live, breathe and strive to fulfill The Prime Directive. That holy, and most revered drive has been getting lost in the ebb and tide of societal changes over the last five thousand years, and its diminishing importance in our Tier Three and Tier Four structures is the singular and primary reason for conflicts in our lives. These unnatural conflicts are growing at an exponential rate across our society, and will ultimately be the reason all life on this planet is extinguished.

An individual organism's existence is not to serve the family. An individual organism's existence is not to serve society. An individual organism's existence is not to own expensive cars and housing. An individual organism's existence is not to travel the world, or to save the whales, or to pay taxes to a government, or to explore space. It is only to survive. The rotting and stinking heap of human societal refuse that is the end result of our isolation from The Prime Directive and who we are as an animal, is now fully laid upon the shoulders of the individual. Only through a total and utter rejection of our modern world experience and current societies can our organism survive. It is only through a re-acquaintance with and commitment to our natural selves can we hope to escape with our lives.

We, as an organism are not a complicated species. Look no further than any television program about the "natural world" and we can talk our lead from any one of the hundreds of thousands of other cell creatures.

I can hear several of you snickering right now, sitting in your homes with great views, in affluent and relatively safe neighborhoods. You ask, "Why in the world would I give up a great earning job, a trophy wife or husband, credit cards, great cars, vaccinations, modern surgery, societal status, and this killer house? What does living in a dirt hole and digging for grubs have over all that modern society has to offer me?"

It's very simple my friend. The world that our societies have built is not sustainable. Not only is it not sustainable, but also our homo sapien societies now threaten the existence of every other species on Earth. Without all these other creatures (the ones without Visa cards) we cannot live. This is a no brainer. Let's take one tiny little nuance to people, the Apis mellifera Linnaeus. Also known by its common name, the European honeybee. Honeybees have been around for one hundred million years and showed up not long after our species transitioned into the great species that it is today. And like our ancestors, its growth and migratory patterns follow our ancestors as they walked across Asia, the Bering Straights and towards Phoenix in their search for a 7-11 that was open. The lives and outcomes of both our two species are so intrinsically tied together, and at such a vital and important level that major events in one of our lives, will have long lasting, and serious effects upon the others. Our species' food chain now fully depends and is completely reliant upon these tiny, annoying, and sometimes threatening little insects. And I will bet dollars to donuts you never once realized that your fancy house, fine car and wines, your credit cards and social status **_all depend_** upon our little friends. Because without the daily help of hundreds of millions of Apis mellifera Linnaeus, flowers don't get pollinated, and food doesn't get grow. And…wait for it…wait…without food our species dies out. Not only that, but without the Honeybee our species could be dead, completely eradicated in less than a single, solar year. There might be a few "Shit Hit the Fan" preppers and hoarders that manage to get past the immediate first wave of mass die off; but our million-year reign as the dominating species on this planet could end in as few as four hundred days. And that year is coming up fast, and you participated in the final solution for our species every single time you swatted at a honey bee, or bought a can of insecticide and went about spraying your house and yard so your beautifully little trophy kids could play out side without those "nasty bugs" chasing after them.

As tied together as the lives of Apis mellifera Linnaeus and homo sapiens are, the consequences of our mutual relationship have never been fully studied or fully appreciated. We, as a species have taken this simple insect completely for granted. And as a result, with the current mass die off and disappearance of the Apis mellifera Linnaeus across the United States and Europe, scientists are scrambling to identify how wide spread the die off actually is. But without having real, solid historical statistical data about the Honeybee's regional and world wide populations, it is all just "best guess" estimates as to whether or not they and we, have passed a tipping point towards a catastrophic conclusion to our long running relationship. And this is only one relationship among millions of relationships in the extremely complex ecosystem of our homo sapien lives on this planet.

Let's taken another example…the Solanum lycopersicum or Tomato plant. It is indigenous to South America and has been domesticated quite recently, about 2500 years ago. The lovely little plant produces a fruit that can be described as both sweet and or bitter depending upon the variety of the plant, and soil and climate it is grown in. And unlike many other vegetables that humans have developed a taste for, its relatively recent introduction into global human diets is proof positive that its DNA and our own body's ability to digest the fruit of the Solanum lycopersicum is compatible. Granted, some may not like the taste, but there are very few reported cases of allergic reaction to this plant. Then in the late 1980's several biotech firms produced the first of a series of Genetically Modified tomatoes. This was done out of need to reduce the damage caused primarily from picking and transportation of the fruit to market. Calgene, the maker of the now infamous GMO "Flavr Savr tomato, released their product in 1993 to a great fan fair of advertising and media attention. Since genetic engineering was only then in its infancy, consumers and growers had many complaints about the taste and ability to live up to Calgene's claims. More importantly, Calgene's researchers underplayed serious safety issues that were discovered in their own clinical experiments with rats. They found, then quietly diminished the fact thin their controlled rat population, "The rats that ate one of these Flavr Savr varieties probably wished they were in a different test group. Out of 20 female rats, 7 developed stomach lesions—bleeding stomachs. The rats eating the other Flavr Savr, or the natural tomatoes, or no tomatoes at all, had no lesions." (By Jeffrey Smith Institute For Responsible Technology Saturday, Jan 1, 2011)

Now I don't mean to discredit the entire field of Genetically Modified Organisms (GMO's) or the many upright and dedicated professionals that work to create these strains. From my perspective, certain GMO's could have a place in our world. I only question the sanity of our species, for the sake of corporations making a dollar, being able to release GMOs into our planet's agricultural food chain. I can't believe that performing one or two clinic lab studies before the introduction of a GMO into the food chain is adequate enough to safeguard our food chain, or our species' ability to digest and use that GMO as a food source. With a few notable exceptions like the Solanum lycopersicum, the food we eat, the food chain, the natural world, and our bodies have spent nearly two million years learning to adapt to one another. For our society to release these GMOs into our world after three lab trials, and *not* dozens of years of experimentation and testing before they are sold cannot be called reckless. It is such a suicidal act that it quickly crosses into the category of global genocide. This is because what we now know about the world we live in is still in its fetus stage.

My third and last example is the development and use of radioactive elements to make electricity and weapons. Without needing to go into a deep level of discussion on the discovery, development and use of radioactivity to power steam generators and make bombs, I assume for brevities sake most reading this will know it. Simply put, for our society to create uranium waste whose toxic and lethal lifespan is not rendered inert in less than two hundred and twenty-five thousand years is beyond words.

These and many other issues like them present our species with our greatest challenges. It is from the fact that our tools and our society's use of those tools is moving and changing at the speed of light. But there is a critical difference between what we are capable of, and what we are capable of understanding and responding responsibly for what we are doing, and that gap is so vastly far apart that the two sides can no longer see the other.

If you are thinking I am a tree hugger and climate change advocate, think again. I love trees, and do see a change in weather trends. But I know that we don't know enough about our own lives, the world, and the countless lives around us to know what is really going on. We simply don't have the mind to understand what we are seeing. Once again, the reduction of pirates across time does not necessarily indicate global warming, (correlation is not causation.)

I also know and believe that our lives, our families, our societies, and the natural world are all out of balance with who we are and what we do. Our long life spans which in turn change our family relationship, which in turn change our societal relationships which in turn put pressure on the individual, which then changes our family structure…etc.

Combines with our creeping increase in the dynamic use of tools in our lives have added a dimension to our lives, but to the natural world itself. And again, none of this is sustainable in the numbers of our species that we now have on the planet. Being the pragmatic person I am, I don't care about how we got here, only how to deal with the reality of where we are.

And to that end, I have written this treatise to help me intellectually flesh out a practical means for us to return to equilibrium. Before I do this, I want to first explore a few specific examples of how being out of balance has manifested in our lives. This will help you to understand what is broken, so in the end chapters I conclude with my blueprint for our next family and social structures, it will make more sense to you. So in the meantime, through that can of bug spray away. It might just push off the day you and your family die of starvation… by a day or two.

CHAPTER SIX - LOVE

The singer Tina Turner once sang, "What's love got to do with it?" And she was right, love is really just a "second hand emotion"

What is popularly called love, is simply a electrical-chemical reaction in the brain that is produced in order to ensure that our species finds a mate, breeds with a mate, and stays with that mate until the off spring can head out of the house (hopefully) and begin breeding on its own. Countless writers have written volumes about romantic love, plutonic love, love unrequited, and love done me wrong, over the last three thousand years. The need for our organism to produce such a strong and passionate need to be with a partner is indicated in the preponderance of love themes in our current society. Entire financial industries have sprung up clambering to repeat profits from this once aspect of our organism's need to mate.

I start Part Two of this book with love, since without that component of human behavior our species would never have made it out of the Savanna of Ethiopia. Without the organism having a mechanism built deep inside us that drew the male and female together, that ensured that they mated, that then kept the young family together through thick and thin, through hunger and thirst we would have quickly perished.

We can read the teachings of Socrates and Plato, of Shakespeare and Burns and of all the world's other great authors, scientists, researchers, and thinkers and still not know what causes love, what continues love, what diminishes love from an organic perspective. Yet, this sole aspect of being human has affected every human life that has ever existed or will exist. And neither our sciences, nor our philosophies can predict who a person will fall in love with. So complex is the matrix of conditions that cause the emotion that legitimate areas of research into the subject of what causes love are currently being done in chemistry, endocrinology, anthropology, neurology, sociology, spirituality, theology, and even astronomy.

Love is so vital to our species and organism that analysis of the five thousand plus years of written language all recount and describe love and the many dimensions of the subject and is the most predominate of all human subjects. Contemporary music, film, literature, television, short stories and fiction are written in abundance to this fundamental biological drive. Quotations about love fill the majority of books in the library, and can be found across the ages of human history.

But what is it?

It is The Prime Directive made manifest in our lives. It is the sand and clay, the rock and limestone of our very existence. And since the driving desire to be with another person that love precipitates, it really matters not for the purpose of this discussion what the root cause ultimately is, only *that it does happen*   ! For our species to survive, love occurs and out of it, the magnificence and magic of our continued survival is allowed to happen one more day.

Ms. Helen Fisher has written four excellent books on love and continues to do research into the intricate chemistry that goes on in the mind of those in love (and out of love) and her body of work points not to a single point of stimulation, but to a broad and clearly defined matrix of what creates love on a biological level. A few of the conditions that trigger the love response are: Good looks, appropriate timing between the couple, socio-economic similarities, and commonalities in education, religion, and lastly reproductive goals. Behind these external conditions are four chemicals that help, in the appropriate levels to create that feeling, that wonderful feeling of love. At the top of the list is Dopamine, Serotonin, Oxytocin, and the two hormones Testosterone, and Estrogen.

For its part Dopamine is considered the drug most associated with being happy. Oxytocin is often called the female cuddle hormone since it is produced in larger quantities in the female than in the male and it helps the female to bond. Serotonin helps the brain to control our moods. It is this drug that many anti-depressants try to help the brain to build up levels of in depressed people. Lastly there are the two primary sex hormones, Testosterone in the male, and Estrogen in the female. These chemicals are the prime growth hormones that are at their peak in the human life cycle form age 9- 22. After about the twenty second year, both male and females levels of the hormones begin their gradual reduction.

You can see that for the feeling of "love" to take place in our species, a very complex set of social, physical, and chemical conditions must come into alignment. A very clear example of this would all have to come together is: Let's look at a male and female whose timing allowed them to be on an E Train into New York City at the same time, and in the same rail car. By chance, by fates, or by the grace of God they end up seating across from one another. Both are of the same socio-economic class, similarly educated, of the same race and both single, with their bodies crying out to fulfill The Prime Directive. They look across the isle and just happened to make contact at the very same time. That moment of magic immediately happens for the male. The Dopamine kicks in, Serotonin levels are normal, and being a healthy twenty-three-year-old male, he is all Testosterone. And like her male counterpart the female has been having dreams of being pregnant for the last four menstrual cycles. But just four days ago, she was fighting off a bad cold, and subsequently, the Serotonin level in her brain is abnormal and she suffers from a mild case of depression. She stares weakly into the blue eyes of her future husband and father of her children for a very brief second, then looks back down to her Iphone and continues reading about Kim Kardassian. The encounter all happens in less than a second, and the lives of both people are NOT changed forever. Mating does not occur and the complex conditions of "Love" must be reproduced time and time and time, in order for all conditions necessary for the "trigger" we call love to propel us, and our species toward replication.

Adding to this complexity is the fact that our family and social structures have now grown so large in population and subsequently dysfunctional, that it becomes harder and harder for individuals to find an appropriate mate that meets the demands to mate. Ms. Fisher is working with a nationally known mating website to do more research on the subject, but simply matching external traits for the two mating partners will never work by itself. Having mutually similar interests mean nothing if the chemicals are in balance in one's mind, and in the mind of the potential mating partner. When families have cohesive structures, and the greater societies represented a commonality, (rather than a diversity of family structures,) finding suitable mates was and is much easier. In many family and social structures the parents traditionally found their children mates based on the social class of the family. Often this practice involved interviewing the other person for suitability for inclusion into their family structure as well. This did, and in many countries still does happen today, and it takes a tremendous burden off the child to find an appropriate mate, given the lack of emotional and social maturity of the child would normally prohibit them from seeking out any mate on their own. Many of my friends who have arranged marriages tell me that "Love" does indeed eventually inter into their relationship through time. You can see from this instance, that the family structure has replaced a key component in the love matrix, which still leads to mating and procreation. Judging from the over population of India, arranged marriages apparently do not damper any part of the couple's biological drive to mate even slightly. Which is great! Is shows that family structures can and do compliment our organism's drive to fulfill The Prime Directive.

Contrary to this example, is the sad fact that more often now that not our family structure is under such a continued attack from greater society needs and demands as to have become impotent in the art and science of successfully raising off spring to adulthood. Look no further than the high crime rates of most American inner cities. Presently Chicago experiences an average of five shootings every single day. Just last year in 2014, there were over 1600 people shot in that city, and over 500 of those victims killed. Across America murder numbers continue to skyrocket every day due to the breakdown in Tier Three and Four structures.

To underestimate the stress that our current societies place upon The Prime Directive is to ignore the fact that these socially induced stressors have become contradictory to our organism's sole reason to live. All tools, all families, all family rituals, and certainly all societies must serve The Prime Directive. Knowing that The Prime Directive is to mate should be put into major focus when dating takes place. When you date, you must date only those people that represent the best of the best for our species. Cast aside all inferior and weak mates. Don't even joke about dating a person who is of poor health or limited intellect. Don't ever become intimate with a person who can't hold a job or is unemployed. Your most sacred responsibility to the survival of our organism is to pick the best mate you can, before becoming intimate and mating. Pick the strongest, youngest, best looking female you can. Pick the male that is the biggest and most financially secure that you can. When we walk into Walmart we should never again see fat, ugly, dirty, unshaven men and women, in torn and tattered clothes with a gaggle of children. Families who allow individual members to mate with inferior people we have produced generations of imperfect and lazy children.

Love as we now know and describe it, is nothing more than the externally defined drive to act upon The Prime Directive. Knowing this, I would hope it would help you respond to the seemingly "uncontrollable" urges you have to mate with more foresight and thought. Mating is not the problem. Mating without the necessary and appropriate tools and family structure in place to support the growth of the child to adulthood is the primary problem our generation faces.

CHAPTER SEVEN - MARRIAGE

"FIRST COMES LOVE, THEN COMES MARRIAGE, THEN COMES CHILD IN A BABY CARRIAGE"

Marriage is for one thing, and only one thing. It is for providing a safe haven in which to grow children. It is not, and never has been a means for young women to live out their fantasies of being a princess. It is not about who spends the most on the wedding ceremony, or how long the bride's dressing gown's train is. It is not about four layer cakes that cost tens of thousands of dollars, and it certainly is not about flying thirty of the family's closest friends to the Cayman Islands for a week. It is not about the man proving how worthy he is to be married to, by spending a year's wage on a ring.

In Roman times, the ritual of marriage (for all classes other than noblemen) was only considered necessary once a child had been produced. Once a woman became impregnated, rules of society demanded that they be brought into the world in a house with the parents. This shows that as late as two thousand years ago that Tier

Three family structures were set up in accordance with The Prime Directive, aka natural law. Roman families and community values were a natural outcropping of TPD. They allowed for the Alpha male to satisfy his need to mate, knowing that not every mating attempt led to conception. Poor sanitation, malnutrition, genetically inferior partners, limited medical knowledge, and disease filled the gap between pregnancy and the lack of working contraception options failed. So it was that many women who allowed themselves to respond to their own body's urge to mate, never successfully brought the fetus to term. This naturally kept the human population numbers down.

The ritual of marriage for the lower classes was instituted for the sake of the survival of the child. That is the only thing that marriage is for. It is not about providing a safe landing for women who have no career goals. It is not about white picket fences and the wife spending all day at the gym while the husband works himself into an early grave. It's not about having a trophy wife for your middle age golf buddies to drool over. It is not a substitute for the father to participate in his own child's life. When it comes to marriage, there is so much wrong with today's family structure that I could write an entire book on this one issue. The sole rational for two people to be contractually bonded together is for the sake of raising their own children. Notice that nowhere in that sentence can you find anything to do with the United States Internal Revenue Tax code. As mentioned previously, the recent US Supreme Court decision that states that homosexuals can get married shows how far modern day societies have gotten from The Prime Directive. Now, I've lived and worked in San Francisco's gay community. My oldest and best friend of over 40 years is a gay man. I have no ill will towards any gay person (who doesn't deserve it!) But for a Tier Four Society structure to mandate laws that authorize two men, or women to marry is just ridiculous. It serves no purpose other than to legitimize certain behavior as a political favor.

The house of marriage is only built to support child rearing. Further, it is not built and should not be built around the need of the abandoned children. Adoption took place as far back as Rome to upper class households that had no male heir. It was only after the Catholic Church had gained dominance in Europe in the 1500's that the idea of adopting a homeless child for the sake of the child, rather than a potential benefit of the adult came into being.

The reason and justification of marriage to our organism is further being corrupted by the Society Structure. With the introduction of laws over the last one hundred years that allow for divorce of a married couple to take place, it undermines the one true necessity and benefits of what a married house provides our off spring. Not only does modern day divorce allow the two parents a quick and easy out to their original decision to procreate, it gives weakens the family structure & marriage relationship while it is still operational and in tack. It was social states that decreed that divorce was allowable for social reasons rather than biological ones. It does this by allowing both adults to know, long before the vows of marriage are taken, that there is an emergency escape cord that can be pulled at any time and without fault. This frees the lame and lazy from any responsibility for their choice of mates, from their failure as individuals to modify anti-social behaviors in the relationship, and from most nearly every offense and short-coming they bring into and maintain in the relationship from affecting them. Divorce gives these people, whose own parents failed to raise them with any real understanding of The Prime Directive an out where there should never be one. Rather than being in a life long committed relationship and the inertial of that situation forcing the couple to actually work through the hundreds of small, and petty issues that come up in the course of living together, it gives them a "Get Out of Jail Free" card. That escape cord is now pulled in over 50% of all marriages. And by having pulled it, leaves the child without a home, or the necessary family structure to live in accordance with natural law. There is no weaker and dysfunctional of a male child, than that who has been raised by a divorced or unmarried woman. Creating laws that allow a couple to divorce was intended solely to allow mature males to return to the mating process. What can I say? Divorce was only legalized by and for middle-aged men who wanted to get back in the game, who wanted to continue having sex and couldn't since they were "legally" married. Once again, it was the Catholic Church that prohibited sex out of marriage. To ensure that the rights of the first-born could easily be determined and in turn, they would inherit property, monogamy was and still is promoted. Pre-Christian societies understood the natural need of men to have sex with more than one partner throughout his life. As a result, most Pagan societies allowed the men to bring young women (and men!) into their marriage home to satisfy that male's sexual appetite. For those women whose first husbands were killed or died, another man was allowed to bring her and her children into his marriage house for the benefits of his sexual appetites, and for the betterment of her children and the social structure they lived in.

Once females have given birth, their estrogen, progesterone and androgen levels drop precipitously, and quickly become non-sexual beings whose sole focus is the infant child, not the husband's sexual needs. Ancient societies understood that unlike the female after childbirth, the male's hormone levels do not drop. Extra marital affairs were common practice in Pagan societies and satisfied the sexual need for the males, while keeping the "home" intact for the sole purpose of ensuring the child grew to adulthood. With the advent of divorce, this has all changed. Additionally it is the prime cause for the subsequent deterioration of the family structure, and with that, the deterioration and destruction of the benefits of a family raising a child. And while many of the Roman family and social rituals around marriage have become part of our modern day marriage rituals, they have been corrupted by two thousand years of religious and governmental societies. The traditional and long standing family structure, based on The Prime Directive was subverted all for the sake of the political body.

All that I have to do to prove I am right in this matter is to read the local news. Everywhere there is violence in communities; there are broken family structures. Every city where the dead are counted in the morning, there are broken families. Every country that is in civil war, there are broken families. Every community where there is genocide, there are broken families. Every nation where there is tyranny, there is broken families. For every single woman with children on welfare and food stamps, there is a broken family.

Across the globe, the lives of young children are thrown into chaos by societies that allow couples to make terrible mating decisions, and then back out of marriage later when times get hard. Fathers go off to work and never to return, leaving their wives and children abandoned and to the mercy of fate, all because they have a biological need for more sex than their worn out wife can or will give him. Children who grow up without both parents grow up wild and without emotional restraint or morality. Families where both parents must work to pay their bills, leave the children unattended, and subsequently unloved. As more and more individuals go through these types of homes, each subsequent generation moves farther and farther away from The Prime Directive. As more people grow up without of the benefits of a marriage home, it forces our larger, Tier Four Societies to play the role of that traditional family structure. Look no further than the current Welfare system in the USA. The Federal Government is now called the "Nanny State" because it houses the single mothers and their children. It feeds the abandoned family, it provides health care, it provides police for safety, it provides transportation to appointments, it provides mental health counseling, it provides laws to govern the children's behavior and even funds and builds institutions that house and punish the abandoned children when they break the rules. These are all duties of adult male in the family structure. They are not duties that our societies should ever be performing. All this becomes a vicious circle where a very small percentage of families are broken, and out of what I believe to be a sincere desire to affect positive change in those family's lives then society steps into the role of family adult. I honestly believe that former United States President Lyndon Johnson wanted to end hunger and poverty in our country and thought through aggressive social policies he could. But when our society provides these goods and services, the society then needs more money from taxpayers to provide the services they are performing, which in turn causes the need for more taxes to be raised, when in turn puts more pressure to survive on the family structures that are still functional, which breaks those down even further. And on and on and on it goes. It is without a doubt a complex cycle with many variables. But this cycle can be broken in one generation.

1. Create private sector jobs to replace welfare.
2. Eliminate the entire welfare system.
3. Eliminate all current government structures.
4. Eliminate all tax agencies.
5. No more credit is to be issued or extended.
6. Eliminate all Banks, and Central Banks.
7. If you can't walk there, you can't work there.
8. Learn what a hammer is for, no more mortgages.
9. Wait until the age 30 to have children.
10. Both parents must have a High School Dipolma.
11. Pick the best mate very carefully, they will last forever.
12. All Pregnancies require a license.
13. Have no more than 2 children before age 35.
14. Abort all defective children and unlicensed pregnancies.
15. Parents who produce a deformed/disabled first child can no longer be licensed to produce.
16. No children after age 35.
17. No licenses will be issued to parents with a history of crime, drugs, obesity and or alcohol abuse.
18. Divorce/separation is not an option.
19. Grandparents must live with new couple.

20. Allow for male sexual needs.
21. If one mate dies, remarry immediately.
22. Children may not be raised by a single parent.
23. The family is *always* responsible for the behavior of any particular individual family member.
24. The entire family will be held accountable for crimes of the individual.

Simple rules for a simple organism.

The Prime Directive is for our organism to survive to adulthood, and couldn't be any simpler. I am certain that you even know of examples of in your own life, in your families and society that we have all moved so very far from this simple requirement.

I ask you now, what have you done in your own life to add to this fatal spiral?

CHAPTER EIGHT - CHILDREN

Dr. David Walker

In 1998 I attended a baby naming ceremony at the Los Angeles Church of Religious Science. The pastor officiating was Dr. David Walker and in the fifteen minutes I sat listening to him, it changed my life. In those few moments intended to introduce the child to the parent's world and friends, Dr. Walker stated: "This child was born whole perfect and complete. He was not born with sin, nor does he require fixing. He is a complete human being. It is then the responsibility of those who have gathered here today, to care for him, and to share with him how the world works. And most importantly, allow him to be the spiritual being, the man that he is."

It occurred to me then, and my research over the past 18 years has confirmed to me, that we have everything we need to be successfully at life buried deep within us. We carry in our DNA the tools, the ability, the body, the drive and the means to build our world out of the nothingness that is the landscape of our human lives. Unlike the thousands of other life forms that have lived on this planet, we, and we alone have the ultimate ability, the innate ability to adapt to the great degree that we do.

Our species has the greatest tool that any life has ever been given. The tool of reason and logic, memory and forecasting. Combined, these tools have propelled us out of our humble beginnings in Africa and across the globe. This month, as I write this book, one of our tools (the NASA spacecraft New Horizons) have traveled three billion miles to the farthest reaches of our own solar system and sent back pictures of the planet Pluto.

The New Horizon's spacecraft is such an extraordinary accomplishment for our species that it is easy to believe that human kind has actually, truly evolved up and away from our ancestors. We willingly allow our egos to play tricks with our own thinking, by the mistaken belief that our tools represent the evolution of our species, rather than that of our species development and revolution of our tools. Our ability to adapt is not a biological carte-blanch to change our basic core of who we are and what we do.

Coming back to the child's baby naming ceremony; He will be the same human being if he grows up playing with a stick and wheel, an erector set, or a Playstation. He has no choice in the matter, and though environment and tools may change his mental hardwiring and affect his personality, it does not change The Prime Directive or the related drivers that are put in place by our organism to survive. As awed as I personally am by the pictures being sent back from the New Horizon's flight past Pluto, they do not change the billions of codes hidden in our DNA. Neither do they change how we live our daily lives as a result of that primal code, nor do the production of these amazing photos change the DNA of our future ancestors any more that any other external influencers do.

Some may contend that our tools represent changes to our most intimate nature.

To those I ask these questions;

- o Has the development of the circular table saw changed the human need for shelter?
- o Has the development of large-scale farming operations changed a human's need for nourishment?
- o Has the development of the atomic bomb changed a human's need for security?
- o Has the development of non-violent families on the planet changed the amount of violence and aggression other people demonstrate?
- o Has the growth and development of the marriage industry changed the female's desire to be impregnated?
- o Do changes in the mind of an adult from using modern tools, change their DNA?

The Prime Directive's requirement is that once the female gives birth to a new organism, the organism must survive. In order for this to happen in a hostile world, the organism developed hormones that acted on the brain; that in turn caused a Paternal/Maternal instinct to protect the off spring through adulthood.

It is at this point that differences to the family structure are seen developing. In Northern Europe we see the

Nuclear family structure come into play, and in most of
Africa and Asia, we see Nomadic / Tribal family structures
develop. Keeping in mind that weather , food availability,
and landscape played a significant role in the development
of the two stereotypical families structure. Families living
in the Europe of ten thousand years ago were able to
remain relatively stationary due to a proliferation of
protein from animals and nuts and berries. It was about this
time that humans began taking advantage of the long
grass-wheat that grew in the region, which then added to
the permanence of their communities. Compare this to
what we now know about the people in current day Qatar.
As recently as 60 years ago there was only a very small
fishing village at Madinat Al Shamal. The village's
population would swell to around 500 in Peril season, but
then drop down to a few dozen when the temperatures
went above 40 Celsius. No food or water and no
community. People can't stay where they can't eat. The
millions of immigrants attempting to enter the United
States every year from South and Central American prove
this out. But along with the need to constantly move to
find food and water came a decidedly distinct family trait.
When people must travel from one place to another
looking for food, for water, and for employment that lack
of physical security causes them to be highly aggressive
and violent. The less secure and more threatening the
external world is, the more negative affect that has on the
structure of the family and its members.

   Living in a world where there is no security of any
kind, other than that which the family structure provides,
has the chilling affect of keeping all members of the family
on an emotional high alert. And that in turn affects every
interaction with the greater society. Every sound, every

situation, every person is a threat. That lack of family and societal structure security produces hyper vigilance and is manifested by the individual in paranoia, quick tempers, hyper aggressiveness, and explosive violence. The further the family structure deteriorates toward chaos, the farther the individual's biological drive responds to it and the need for the organism to survival at all costs comes to the forefront. In situations like this, the individual's dependency upon the family remains, but the ability of the child to grow intellectually, mature naturally, and become an adult capable of properly raising a child of its own is destroyed.

Nuclear families who experience a reduction or destruction of their food supplies undergo even more extreme reactions to this scenario, and have often become extremely territorial and aggressive. Take for instance the Vikings. The people in the region were relatively benign and non aggressive up until the mid-sixth century. But the climate in Northern Europe cooled off (long before the invention of the automobile:) and within a hundred years the people of Scandinavia had become the aggressive fighters that we now call Vikings. Accounts of the change in weather were recorded by a number of writers of the period.

Flavius Cassiodorus wrote about conditions that he experienced during the year AD 536: "The Sun seems to have lost its wonted light, and appears of a bluish colour. We marvel to see no shadows of our bodies at noon, to feel the mighty vigour of the Sun's heat wasted into feebleness, and the phenomena which accompany an eclipse prolonged through almost a whole year. We have had a summer without heat. The crops have been chilled by north winds, [and] the rain is denied."

Procopius : "...*during this year a most dread portent took place. For the Sun gave forth its light without brightness...and it seemed exceedingly like the Sun in eclipse, for the beams it shed were not clear.*"

Lydus : "*The Sun became dim...for nearly the whole year...so that the fruits were killed at an unseasonable time.*"

Michael the Syrian : "*The Sun became dark and its darkness lasted for eighteen months. Each day it shone for about four hours, and still this light was only a feeble shadow...the fruits did not ripen and the wine tasted like sour grapes.*"

It should not be surprising then that families across the globe, when faced with changing circumstance become hostile, aggressive, and violent. But we can see that those who exist in relatively stable climatic or food supply conditions show a marked decrease in the need to exert the inherent violence we are capable of. But even in current societies where the food and weather are stable we see violence. Though food may be plentiful families can still be under stress. Stress from external foes, stress from internal changes, stress from societal changes. Any and all stressors, real or perceived, that challenge the organism's ability to survive puts stress on it and the family structure. Any family where the father has lost his job and money becomes scarce, knows what this is like. In today's war torn societies like Syria, families are torn apart by the bombs and killing that goes on daily. Entire populations off Syrian towns have moved into Turkey, Europe, Jordan,

Qatar and even the United States. The children of these families will grow up more violent, more aggressive and hostile toward other tribes and societies. This is turn will perpetuate the next and next conflicts in the region. It is a self fulfilling prophesy that those who live by the sword, die by the sword, and their children, and children's children.

Genghis Khan lived in the thirteenth century and was an ancestor of Asiatic rulers dating back to the year 2100 bce. In those three thousand years his family line was filled with dozens of military leaders and rulers. Genghis sired several hundred children of his own lifetime with countless women, both in marriage and with slaves that he captured. That lineage now lives on in modern day China and Mongolia with over eight hundred million people alive who all descended from just eleven of Genghis' family. Is it no wonder then that so many of these dynasties (Tier Four Social Structures) have such remarkable reputations for violence and mayhem?

In societies where there is tremendous competition for that food only the most aggressive person was able to survive. Once again it is The Prime Directive driving family and social structures.

Coming back to Dr. David Walker's remarks. "A child is born whole perfect and complete." He was speaking of the spiritual aspect of the child. I, of course, am speaking of the organism itself. Whether it is the organism's primal need to survive, or the social structure that the child is born into, or a specific DNA that causes our species wanton and naked aggression we know to be present in our species.

We could spend an entire lifetime debating on whether it is the chicken or the egg that came first. What matters is not the cause, but the response to it. And that response can only be fixed by having stable family structures. It can only happen by insisting that our Tier Four social structures produce and have as little affect upon the individual and family as is possible. If living in a society, a city, or country produces such stress upon individuals that they live in a constant state of "flight or fight" then it has lost it primary purpose and should be abandoned to wild dogs and feral pigs. There is little doubt that our modern society has grown to such a monolithic size that it is nearly uncontrollable. Its demand for resources, both financial and in servitude now completely overshadows the role of the family. Even the most severe and authoritarian society can never replace the myriad of benefits that the family provide the individual child.

Children need safe families. Families don't need societies.

CHAPTER NINE - SEXUALITY

In all fairness to my many gay friends, I could not finish out this work without touching, however briefly, on how sexuality fits into The Prime Directive. It is clear from the most elementary understanding of our species, that if we cut through all of the fashion magazines, interior design, social institutions, politics, space programs and iterations of modernizations of our tools, we are still nothing more than an organism, amongst many hundreds of thousands of other organisms on the planet seeking to survive the rigors of life.

That is it. Finito, Hallas, Nada Mas, ei mitään, ingenting, ingenting, inte, ekkert, niente , ikke, niet, semi…No more.

Any anyone that tries to tell you that our lives are not controlled by biology, or that our intellect has elevated us beyond the brutality of our ancestors is smoking crack cocaine. Don't believe a single word they are spewing out from their coke driven haze. Which brings us to sexuality. Our sexual drive, from an purely organism perspective, is solely for the purpose of driving males and females together for the sake of mating. And any other sexual drivers do not serve that purpose. Bondage / Dominance, Sado-masochism, fetishism, homosexuality, bi-sexuality, transsexualism, dressing in diapers, dressing as French maids (I have a _great_ story about a guy I met in a shoe store in West Hollywood buying shoes for his French maid outfit! But that's another story!) and all the other manifestations that are attached to the desire and need to have orgasms or sexual release are all inconsequential to our species' survival. Period.

Don't you find it the least bit suspicious that the Supreme Court of the United States ruled that homosexuals could marry? How does that possibly serve the people of the twenty-eight states that passed laws that clearly stated marriage is between a man and woman? How can this ruling by five un-elected lawyers make our society better? And if everyone is so concerned with our children being raised in better homes, wouldn't a reduction of the tax burden by 100% on all families with children in them, improve their lives more than this blanket approval for homosexuality? It would, but since the ruling class in America wants to distract us all from the cliff we are now facing, they threw the dog a bone rather than allow us to see behind the current.

In the scheme of things, it matters not a fig whether or not a million or two million people in the United States are same-sex attracted. That is less than a third of 1% of the population. It would actually be better for us if 95% of the world were to turn to homosexuality. But that is only my personal daydream and will never happen. (Less people is good, more people is bad.) And to this point, we must understand that as an organism, much like a mother duck with a dozen little ducks, organisms know that something is off about another organism that is intrinsically different from it. That is why homosexuals will always be outcasts in human societies. They are different and though they may look the same, other people can tell, on some level that the closeted gay person is somehow…not the same. Right now there is much press about a former athlete named Bruce Jenner. Bruce recently came out as a transsexual and the American press has been having a field day with the news. Before Jenner, there was Jan Morris, and Christine Jorgensen and many others who've undergone Sex Reassignment Surgery. But I've got bad news for her and all the other people who change their sex. Once they come back from Thailand, or wherever they are performing the surgery these days, they will never fit into society. Not in the US, not in France and not anywhere else. Organisms have one goal, and have evolved into two sexes, A or B. Not A and plastic surgery and a good makeup guy in Brentwood. And all the other organisms know deep in their bones that you are somehow different. Not A, and not B.

And that's okay, but gays, lesbians, and transsexuals must understand from this moment forward, that there really is nothing wrong with their choices, but that those choices distance them from being included in the perpetuation of our species. I have yet to meet a gay person that doesn't understand that. Yet there has been this misguided movement in the United States to prove that gay and lesbian relationships are just as "valid" as heterosexual. This is clearly not the case. Having a government agency give a gay couple a piece of paper does not change the fact that their relationship is operating outside of The Prime Directive. Projecting a gay multicolor flag on the outside of the White House does not change the very nature of that relationship to the organism. Our organism wants one thing… to replicate. These gay "marriages" are political in nature and have zero impact on the state of things.

I of all people fully understand this. But had I understood this when I was in my reproductive years, I don't know if I would have made the same decisions as I did. I keep putting off the opportunity to have children. I kept using money, relationships, work, drug addiction, and a host of other excuses to put off having a family, and I never did have any children. These excuses that many lesser and more stupid people in our society never considered before getting pregnant. Now that I am sixty and can more fully appreciate what this life is all about, I feel left out of the real meaning of why I am here.

This angst, is nothing more than me, as an organism telling me…I should have spawned.

United States Supreme Court 2015

CHAPTER TEN - VIOLENCE

Countless philosophers, intellects, poets, sociologists, and leaders through the ages have all asked what causes violence, aggression and war. I am not the first person to deep at this deep-rooted scar in attempting to identify why our species is so prone to acts of physical aggression. And it is good that people ask, and continue to ask why our species, and not any others behave in such a manner. The wake and costs that violence wreaks upon society is staggering. There is the medical cost to repair the people damaged by it, the social services and police cost to respond to incidents, the cost in lost productivity by those affected by it, the damaging effects to any children that are exposed to it, the loss of security to the individuals, the families, and society. And this is just related to a man who assaults his wife. Should the violence be regional instead, the entire physical infrastructure of the country can be destroyed in a matter of hours, as was the case in Iraq in 2002 when the United States invaded that country. As of this writing in 2015, that country has yet to be able to rebuilt its electrical and water distribution system to the same level as pre-US invasion levels. During state sponsored violence, entire populations are displaced and end up moving hundreds or thousands of miles to be clear of the violence. This in turn destroys communities they came from and the ones that move to. The humanitarian costs in Syrian after four years of civil war are now estimated to be $78 billion dollars. Violence, whether it is in the Englewood section of Chicago during a drive by shooting, the twenty thousand Swedish women who are raped by Muslim men each year, or the sixteen thousand murders each year in South Africa, or by Buddhist Monks against Muslims in the North of Myanmar all have their roots in The Prime Directive. The organism must survive and to that end, must have an automatic mechanism built into it whereby threats to its survival are quickly acted upon. The mechanism must be automatic, quick to turn on, allow the organism to survive a fight, and quick to turn off.

The ability of the homo sapien male to get angry at a threat, fight off an attack, survive that attack and then cool off is vital to our species. I don't believe that it mattered to the original design and development if the organism actually lived in such a dangerous world that needed these self-defense programs. They must have been hard coded into the very first model of homo sapiens, since without it there would not have been Homo Sapien version 2.0. How this happened is anyone's speculation, but it is abundantly clear from the recorded history of homo sapien 1.0 that violence, war, murder, assault, rape and robbery happen everywhere we have migrated. Our human mind is clever enough to have imagined a Eutopia, but not clever enough to find a way to rout out that portion of DNA which has the majority of males in our species hard wired with a physical response that keeps the world on the verge of destruction.

It appears that the only way to modify this hair trigger response is to provide the child a stable home environment. Many writers, infinitely more brilliant that I could wish to be have previously been willing to link our biology to criminal behavior. They may even go so far to give a friendly nod in the direction of admitting that our biological drive to mate is a good thing. The say that "Sex is good... so this biology thing can't be all bad, right boys?" But they intentionally avoid linking all of the other good, and bad things that come along with our being an organism. They desperately want us to believe that we as a species have evolved, that our DNA has evolved and as a result, we are not the same brutal, sadistic, violent predatory animal that we were a million years ago. Time and again they say that our criminal behavior is linked to it, that our sex drive is linked to it...but not the rest of our lives. They point out our fancy tools, our Mozarts and Michelangelo's and our Steven Hackings as proof positive that we have risen above the jungle beasts we once were. Having done this, they now are forced conjure up an assortment of rationale and reasons for wars, civil unrest and rapes. Because, you know, we are not the creatures we once were. They illiteracy, poverty, mothers and fathers that didn't love them, they blame racism, and even blame poor nutrition rather than look directly in the eye of what really is. It is so humbling an experience to admit that we are no different than our ancestors that these great thinkers refuse to bend a knee to the truth that is right in front of them.

Even though statistics show Nuclear families show a much-reduced level of violent behavior than do Tribal family and social structures, they do not show an elimination of violence in those societies. These European communities still have their share of rapes, murders, robberies, and white-collar crimes. They still have their fair share of alcoholism, drug, and child abuse. To simply point out that Nuclear families have a greater reduction of these violent attributes does not discount the fact their level is not at zero. I believe that only a level of at or near zero violence in one archetype of family structure would indicate that violence is a byproduct of Tier Three family structures and not endemic of our species.

More importantly is the fact that by ignoring the possibility, however remote, that all (or part) of this murder and mayhem may be a result of The Prime Directive's survival trigger. Let's play in this sandbox for a little while, shall we? Let's say that it is! That all of this murder, these drive by shootings, the rape of eighty year old women, the civil wars, the world wars, the bombings, the IEDs, the killing people in their sleep, the Norwegian Summer Camp killings, the Jeffery Dahmers, and Jack the Rippers are all a result of our DNA and The Prime Directive. Then what? If there is no current way of changing our DNA and TPD, then it would appear that we might as well give up now and collectively roll over and die. "Cry Havoc, and let slip the dogs of war," said Shakespeare. Yes, and we should let slip the dogs of war, because the way we have been trying to suppress and deny our primordial urges is just not working. But as our populations grow larger and larger, our families have given up the hope of every controlling their own children's biological urges and have pushed off the responsibility to the society structure.

This is from the Steven Sondheim play, West Side Story.

Dear kindly Sergeant Krupke,
You gotta understand,
It's just our bringin' up-ke
That gets us out of hand.
Our mothers all are junkies,
Our fathers all are drunks.
Golly Moses, natcherly we're punks!
Gee, Officer Krupke, we're very upset;
We never had the love that ev'ry child oughta get.
We ain't no delinquents,
We're misunderstood.
Deep down inside us there is good!
My father is a bastard,
My ma's an S.O.B.
My grandpa's always plastered,
My grandma pushes tea.
My sister wears a mustache,
My brother wears a dress.
Goodness gracious, that's why I'm a mess!

Society, now trying to play surrogate parent to
hundreds of millions of off spring is forced to impose the
leash upon everyone in hopes of reigning in and
controlling everyone's personal urges. But parents forget
about the fact that the new holder of our leashes, is also
one and the very same animal as the dog they are trying to
control, and those "leaders" intentionally let our young and
innocent youth off the leash just long enough to wage
violence on their personal (societal) behalf. Under the new
world order that we now live our youth die and don't even
know what they died for.

The urge to protect the organism, the mate, the child, the family, and the neighborhood is <u>GOOD</u>. The urge for males to play rough and be hyper physical is a <u>GOOD THING.</u>

It is only when these urges are suppressed or redirected in inappropriate directions that they become volatile, toxic and destructive to the entire social structure. It is only when there is not a solid family structure in place for each child that things begin to go so terribly wrong. The family, through roles, through examples, through experience, and through hard lessons learned help to teach the individual, both male and female what is and is not appropriate to do with these biological urges that all sorts of nasty shit happens. In a nutshell, family structures teach children what it means to be human, and how to operate in the society they live in. This goes back again to what Dr. Walker was saying. "This child was born whole perfect and complete." Our role, as the adults in the child's life, is to show them how they work, how we work, and ultimately how to be the organism that they are; violent, hostile, protective, procreative, adaptive, and resourceful. The ultimate goal for each of us it to accept our (biological, intellectual, and spiritual) selves for who and what we are.

Genghis Khan's family taught he as a child how to utilize his natural biological aggressiveness to the organism's, and his personal full potential… appropriate to the world in which he lived in.

Our violent tendencies are always swinging back and forth like a pendulum. It is the stress and competencies that our families are under that support or reject whatever specific violent level may be appropriate at the time. Without having learned the proper level of violent response for the world they live in, individuals can suffer from both extremes of violence and non-violence. People who are taught by the family to be passive can be trampled over by a hostile world around them, or excel as being in step with the world, if they live in a peaceful situation. And the very reverse can be true. If a family is fearful of retaliation for aggression, then the children may not have the ability to respond properly to other tribal aggressors. If he lives in a relatively safe world, any overt-aggression on his part can be a threat to the family and the community. The expression of violence and aggression should reflect back to the world the family is born into. Scientists who blame the external world for turning a person into a monster, when the world they are born into is monstrous world do the entire field of research into the cause of violence a disservice. To this day, seventy-five years after the rise and fall of the German Third Reich many people have a neurotic, and deep-rooted need to paint Adolf Hitler as a monster of unparallel proportions. Yes, he and his henchmen started a war that left twenty-five million dead. But let's zoom out of 1940 German for just one minute. In the below table produced by www.scaruffi.com we see just how prolific society's Cry Havoc and let slip the dogs of war.

Remember, the follow table *is not a complete list!*

Ze-Dong Mao (China, 1958-61 and 1966-69, Tibet 1949-50)	100million
Adolf Hitler (Germany, 1939-1945)	24,000,000
Leopold II of Belgium (Congo, 1886-1908)	8,000,000
Jozef Stalin (USSR, 1932-39)	75,000,000
Hideki Tojo (Japan, 1941-44)	5,000,000
Ismail Enver (Ottoman Turkey, 1915-20)	1,200,000 Armenians (1915) + 350,000 Greek Pontians and 480,000 Anatolian Greeks (1916-22) + 500,000 Assyrians (1915-20)
Pol Pot (Cambodia, 1975-79)	1,700,000
Kim Il Sung (North Korea, 1948-94)	1.6 million
Menghistu (Ethiopia, 1975-78)	1,500,000
Yakubu Gowon (Biafra, 1967-1970)	1,000,000
Leonid Brezhnev (Afghanistan, 1979-	900,000

1982)	
Jean Kambanda (Rwanda, 1994)	*800,000*
Saddam Hussein (Iran 1980-1990 and Kurdistan 1987-88)	*600,000*
Tito (Yugoslavia, 1945-1980)	*570,000*
Suharto/Soeharto (Indonesian communists 1965-66)	*500,000*
Fumimaro Konoe (Japan, 1937-39)	*500,000*
Jonas Savimbi – but disputed by recent studies (Angola, 1975-2002)	*400,000*
Mullah Omar – Taliban (Afghanistan, 1986-2001)	*400,000*
Idi Amin (Uganda, 1969-1979)	*300,000*
Yahya Khan (Pakistan, 1970-71)	*300,000 (Bangladesh)*
Ante Pavelic (Croatia, 1941-45)	*359,000 (30,000 Jews, 29,000 Gipsies, 300,000 Serbs)*
Benito Mussolini (Ethiopia, 1936; Libya, 1934-45; Yugoslavia, WWII)	*300,000*
Mobutu Sese Seko (Zaire, 1965-97)	*200,000*
Charles Taylor (Liberia, 1989-1996)	*220,000*
Foday Sankoh (Sierra Leone, 1991-2000)	*200,000*

Suharto (Aceh, East Timor, New Guinea, 1975-98)	200,000
Ho Chi Min (Vietnam, 1953-56)	1,200,000
Michel Micombero (Burundi, 1972)	150,000
Slobodan Milosevic (Yugoslavia, 1992-99)	100,000
Hassan Turabi (Sudan, 1989-1999)	100,000
Syngman Rhee (South Korea, 1948-50)	80,000 (various massacres of civilians)
Richard Nixon (Vietnam, 1969-1974)	70,000 (Vietnamese and Cambodian civilians)64,000 American service men
Efrain Rios Montt – but disputed by recent studies (Guatemala, 1982-83)	70,000
Papa Doc Duvalier (Haiti, 1957-71)	60,000
Rafael Trujillo (Dominican Republic, 1930-61)	50,000
Bashir Assad (Syria, 2012-13)	50,000
Francisco Macias Nguema (Equatorial Guinea, 1969-79)	50,000
Hissene Habre (Chad, 1982-1990)	40,000
Chiang Kai-shek (Taiwan, 1947)	30,000 (popular

	uprising)
Vladimir Ilich Lenin (USSR, 1917-20)	30,000 (dissidents executed)
Francisco Franco (Spain)	30,000 (dissidents executed after the civil war)
Fidel Castro (Cuba, 1959-1999)	30,000
Lyndon Johnson (Vietnam, 1963-1968)	30,000
Maximiliano Hernandez Martinez (El Salvador, 1932)	30,000
Hafez Al-Assad (Syria, 1980-2000)	25,000
Khomeini (Iran, 1979-89)	20,000
Robert Mugabe (Zimbabwe, 1982-87, Ndebele minority)	20,000
Rafael Videla (Argentina, 1976-83)	13,000
Guy Mollet (France, 1956-1957)	10,000 (war in Algeria)
Harold McMillans (Britain, 1952-56, Kenya's Mau-Mau rebellion)	10,000
Jean-Bedel Bokassa (Centrafrica, 1966-79)	?
Paul Koroma (Sierra Leone, 1997)	6,000
Osama Bin Laden (worldwide, 1993-2001)	3,500

President Barack Obama drone killings	*5,500*
Augusto Pinochet "the missing" (Chile, 1973)	*3,000*
Combined totals for all of World War I casualties	*37,000,000*
Spanish American War of 1902	*307,000*

As familiar as I am with these numbers, they assault my senses every time I look at them. It is exactly these figures that prove my entire point. Violence is who we are, and it is what we do. Those who proudly proclaim, "Biology is not destiny" need to sit down and read this chart again and again and again until the full scope of what we really are sinks in. These are not just numbers; they are human beings, homo sapiens, living organisms that are murdered by others of their own species. Hundreds of millions of times each century and still counting. And these numbers don't include the daily shooting sprees in Chicago, Philadelphia, Baltimore, Detroit or South Africa. If after reading this chart you still insist that "Biology is not destiny" then go on, keep kidding yourself, but for the love of God, please stop trying to convince the rest of us that we have moved beyond the plains of Ethiopia simple because you have two newly printed tickets for a performance of Gilbert and Sullivan's the Mikado, for next Saturday night in Cambridge.

So, what is the alternative to the mass genocide we perpetuate upon one another?

It starts with acceptance, then for building strong families that temper it, societies that understand and find avenues for it, and individuals that don't allow themselves to act irrationally to stimulus that may trigger it. Everyone has skin in this game, and everyone suffers or is rewarded by getting a handle on the entire perspective of why good people do bad things. Getting back to dear old Adolf, he was not a monster. He was an organism that felt under attack. Go back and read his "Mein Kampf" where he spells it all out twenty years before the start of World War II. "When the territory of the REICH embraces all the Germans and finds itself unable to assure them a livelihood, only then can the moral right arise, from the need of the people to acquire foreign territory. The plough is then the sword; and the tears of war will produce the daily bread for the generations to come." (Adolf Hitler)

If we keep in mind The Prime Directive, then we can clearly see that selfishness is simply an external expression of the organism's need to satisfy itself. And whether that selfishness is for one's family, or one's tribe, or one's community. It is still the same emotion. We all want what we want. Children often don't want to share toys with the other kids. Adults will throw co-workers under the bus in meetings with the boss to protect and deflect their own bad work, and in order to protect their own jobs. Survival that is what it is all about. Survive this job, this relationship, this police stop, this bad economy, this fight, this argument, this civil war, this French aggression, and or this holocaust.

Survive, Survive, Survive.

What I am not saying is that all violence is the same. Certainly, there is a major difference between a person who kills a home intruder in self-defense and a gang of street thugs that just drive around and kill people randomly. The difference is that the former is based upon the organism's need to survive; the later being a manifestation of a failed family and society structure to properly raise the organism, or worse yet, killing an innocent person for the sake of being initiated into a local gang. Then on the extreme edge of this behavior are those sociopaths that kill for the pleasure of killing. I myself enjoy hunting game. And I have felt elation from having successfully hunted dear and other game animals. This elation I believe goes back to the organism's need for food and survival.

From all the accounts of serial killers interviews I've read, it would appear that they derive the same enjoyment, thrill and elation when they kill another person as I do a Quail. They and I, share the same love of hunting, the prime difference is that I hunt to survive; while they hunt humans purely for the emotional release and sense of control it gives them.

I personally don't see where there is a real difference between any of these killings, only the parameters of logic, pathology and justification the different groups attach to the killing.

It is who we are and it is what we do.

Even our laws allow for killing, if only in self-defense. To add to the lunacy behind this issue is that many societies allow for the killing of a person, who kills another person without an "OFFICIAL" justification for the act. To me, that is the ultimate act of insanity that societies suffer from. This logic is so polluted and convoluted that it cannot apply to any other type of crime. Imagine a person caught shoplifting perfume from a store.

They are arrested and upon conviction of that crime, the jury is then forced to go out and shoplift perfume from Macy's department store. Another man robs a bank of ten thousand dollars. After convection, all 12 jurors must go rob banks for the same amount. The fact that we have courts across the world, that condone the killing of murders is simply more proof that we are all biologically driven to defend the organism. It is the non-survival type killing of another organism that is considered abhorrent. It is also the fact that the individual, rather than society that has made the decision to kill that then becomes problematic for the society structures. There is a collective repulsion of "Vigilante" action in societies the world. This is society, pushing back on the natural authority and responsibility of the individual's right to self-determination. I ask you, if a belligerent asshole is killed in the forest and buried in a deep unmarked grave, is it still a crime?

Take a moment and look back at the cover of this book. The photograph, taken by Mr. Eddie Adams on February 1, 1968. This was during the North Vietnam Tet Offensive in during the Vietnam War. South Vietnamese General Nguyen Ngoc Loan is seen executing a North Vietnamese solider. Is General Loan's killing really any different that a Chicago drive-by shooting? There might be a thousand treaties signed by a thousand governments over the centuries on how the parties will properly conduct a war. They spell out how and under what circumstance killing can and can't happen. They explain in great, pain-staking details who and who should not be violated or murdered. And ultimately, they are all ignored. All that really matters is the killing. Killing is King, killing is what we do for frak's sake. It is only when we accept it, that we are willing to bite down into this apple and look God straight in the eye and tell him the truth our having eaten the forbidden fruit that we can finally stand straight in the light of day. We are driven to survive, we are driven to defend, and we are driven to kill that which would destroy us. We have natures expressed right to kill those who threaten us. No questions asked, no trial, no jury, no harm and no foul.

When I watch TV with my friends (more liberal than I) and see crocodiles kill wildebeests in Africa, I have never heard any one of them suggest that the crocodiles be arrested for first-degree homicide. But heaven help the person who uses a handgun to kill an intruder, and my very same friends cry out for the blood of the person who shot the intruder. The two are the same; they both come from an internally driven need to survive. For people to split hairs on this issue, insisting that one is for food while the other is unrelated to survival is to dance in circles. It is only by accepting this sometimes hard truth about own natural instincts can we come to terms with it. Isn't that what all of the Jungian therapists tell us to do? We must accept ourselves for who we are, before we can every hope to change it. And I am certainly not suggesting that all the violence is a bad thing. I believe that society has moved so far out of balance, that there must be a tremendous shift back to center. Our societies are broken, our families are broken, and I fear that it can only return to a normalized state after a painful re-alignment.

As the Joker said in a Batman movie, "This Town needs an enema" And I'm afraid that is what it will take to force society to relinquish its control on the individual and force families to once again take responsibility for raising its own children.

When the first major research of the Karen Hill tribes of
Thailand, Laos, and Myanmar was done in the early 1960s,
researchers made note that members of the tribe lived
communally in a traditional Long House. As you can see
from the photograph, there are no separations, no walls,
and nowhere for a person to have any secrets. At night,
couples might simply put up a one foot high partition when
making love, that only separated them visually from the
other dozen or so family members in the house. All in the
house hear every noise that is made. Privacy, as we know
it in Western societies, is vastly different, and it is not
uncommon for other family members to accompany each
other, or even Western guests to the river when they went
to relieve themselves. It is in this kind of family structure
that deviations and privations from the norm are quickly
seen by another family member and shared/restricted by
the entire family.

On April 20th, 1999 two Colorado teenagers went on a
rampage in their High School killing thirteen people. The

pair later that day committed suicide. According to a New York Times Article dated, April 27, 1999 local police were quoted as saying: *"The Jefferson County Sheriff, John P. Stone, highlighted the attention on the parents of the two gunmen, Eric Harris, 18, and Dylan Klebold, 17. Sheriff Stone said on Saturday that a sawed-off shotgun barrel and bomb-making materials had been found in plain sight in one of the boys' rooms."*

But both of Dylan Klebold's parents knew nothing of the weapons, and confessed to having not been in the room in some time. This kind of deviant social behavior, as well as the planning and material assembly needed to carry it out, would never be possible amongst the Karen Hill tribes. In traditional families' structures, everyone is accountable to the family, and there are few secrets.

My entire premise for this work is that violence is a natural / biological manifestation of the human organism. But with its roots buried in the need for self-defense of the species, rather than a prepubescent & maligned need for revenge against the cute girls in a teenager's school or against street rivals. The final outcome is the same; people are dead, but a few simple rules can be used to validate or invalidate the use of the violent response. At first glance, it may appear that I am splitting hairs on this. Yet it is an inescapable fact that aggressive/violent behavior has its roots in all human DNA. One can ask then, why is it that Genghis Khan and his million predecessors and successors all share the very same hyper aggressive and violent traits, while at the same time, countless millions of people they conquered and subjugated did not? There is an easy explanation to this. The Tier Three and Tier Four structures those subjugated people lived in had developed differently. How agricultural families lived and their collective need for aggression, while they watched the grass grow, is different from the need for aggression for the Khan family of nomadic peoples who had to continue to move and stay fluid like a shark to eat and provide for their own (Khan and friends) family. Coming back to the Columbine High School killers Eric Harris and Dylan Klebold, Their aggression was targeted at the social structure that they inhabited. Their very own school. Once again we see clearly their parents/family influence and moral system had been supplanted by that of the school they attended. The Tier Four Societal structure…ie. Columbine High School became their family. Tier Four institutions now intentionally want and are designed so that the individual look to it, to be all things, to replace the family. American schools now have codes of conduct that no longer reflect those of the families whose children attend them. It is through these strict codes of conduct that the institutions attempt to modify individual behavior to fit the strategic goals of the society, rather than the values and morals of the family. What happened at Columbine and countless other schools, colleges and workplaces over the last twenty years are a backlash to this intentional process of societal indoctrination. This backlash is due to the fact that the institutions can never be designed or function exactly like a small, cohesive family structure can, and is due primarily to the wide diversity of individuals who attend that school. Nazi Germany's institutions were able to carry out their social indoctrination because they operated in homogeneous communities across Germany, whose family structures shared a common set of moral, political and social beliefs that the Third Reich was attempting to push forward with the people at the time.

Harris and Klebold were social outcasts in a system that is completely and utterly ill prepared to identify and effectively deal with deviant anti-social behavior and whose values were different from that of the two shooters. It was World War One that solidified and coagulated the German people's moral belief that the rest of the world was against them. If the war had not done that, then certainly the brutal terms of the Treaty of Versailles ultimately did. In the twenty years after that treaty was imposed upon the Germany, it forged a collective social belief among all the people of that country. The population of German was nearly ninety million people in 1940. And there were only a handful of German protests against the Third Reich in the ten previous years. But those who protested were protesting as Germans, rather than as outcasts like Harris and Klebold. Unlike the racial protests that America has seen in 2015, those German protests never involved arson and the destruction of private property, nor the personal attacks on members of the German police. The violence and looting seen in recent American racial protests is due to the fact that the protestors and the society they protest have different values and morals. This was not the case with protests against the Third Reich in the eight years preceding World War Two.

All acts of aggression/violence must be viewed in the context of where they take place. Adolf Hitler and the German people felt perfectly justified by the Third Reich's invasion and occupation of twenty countries, in retaliation for the insult and suffering they experienced at the hands of British and French at Versailles. United States President Barack Obama has justified the murder of over five thousand people by drone attack, saying they are a threat to the United States. The French in Algeria killed thousands during that country's civil war by saying they were rebels and traitors. Syrian President Assad has waged a war against opponents that has destroyed every city in that country, and believes he is justified because the rebels are terrorists against his government. Columbine killers Harris and Klebold went into their school and killed 13 other students, justifying their actions because of their anger at them. The more we dig at this scab, the more we really see it is all the same. It is all violence, all primal, and all justified by one excuse or the other, isn't it?

    It is Who we are and What we do. After thousands of years of killing and killing and more killing, do we really still need to split this hair? I don't think so. Let's get real on the subject of violence. Let's not split hairs and say this kind of violence is okay, and that other kind, the kind were innocent kids on their way to school get killed is somehow bad. It is who we are and what we do and we will never get past our lies and deceits, and half truths about all of this if we keep pushing the fact that we are a most remarkably violent, aggressive and combative species. We are all killers. We are communities filled with fun loving killers all waiting their turn to find that right and perfect moment to express our primal rage. It is only after the fact, after the slaughter, after the genocide, after the Reichkrystallnacht that we look for reasons to justify our outburst. It is only after the sheer delight from the orgasm of violence, in that post climatic shame we feel, that we try to push off responsibility for our actions and blame the victims, blame our drinking, blame religion, blame our fears, blame their culture. But whether it is Dylan Klebold or Heinrich Himmler, Stalin, Hitler, or Obama it is all the same. We are a violent species always at the ready, always primed to react, to defend, to survive, and to kill.

I would like to introduce a dear friend of mine, Mr. Peter Vacco. For the last twenty-six years Peter has spent most summers hiking across North America. He started at the lower Continental Divide in New Mexico, and every summer gradually walked solo until he reached Alaska. After having thoroughly hiked the fuck out of that State, he then began walking eastward across Canada's section of the Arctic Circle. In April 2015, he walked solo from Kugluktuk, 380 miles across the ice to Cambridge Bay, Nanavut in a record time of 22 days. Over the years Peter has hiked over fifteen thousand miles by himself. At an average speed of 2.2 miles a day that would mean that he has spent over seven thousand hours, (give or take) in self imposed exile and solitude. Peter is a man that has had plenty of time to ponder all things worldly and in great depth.

He would like to remind us at this point in the conversation, that every rule that is put in place to control or limit the parameters of violence is actually one more rule that's in the way of our survival. An excellent example of this are the recent rioting in major cities across America by blacks who are protesting police related shootings in their communities. Police in these communities were actually told by politicians to not respond to rioters and looters and to "Stand Down" for largely political reasons. As a result, entire sections of those communities were destroyed by roaming criminals. Innocent people were murdered and countless stores and home burnt to the ground. By having too many rules and prohibitions in place (regardless of their rationale), the police were not able to respond to acts of aggression in like, and quell the disturbances. History has shown that people will continue behaving in a particular way, until there is sufficient pain to make them rethink what they are doing. The world was never built around the 1867 "Queensberry rules of the sport of boxing." Liberal America society's interpretation of traditional rules of law all presuppose that the world we live in is a controlled boxing arena and that once your opponent lowers his gloves, he is no longer to be considered a threat, a combatant. Let's say that an assailant just beat your innocent mother to death and then turned his back on her lifeless body and walked ten feet away. Let us then say you shoot him in the back, killing him dead. Every single court in this nation would convict you of murder. Based wrongly on the supposition that he was no longer a threat, in that situation. You would be the criminal, not he. The liberal courts, and District Attorney offices all believe that he put down his gloves and were no longer a threat/combatant. But in that brief moment that he turned his back, what were the chances of him having found Jesus? What are the odds that he stopped the attack and had a change of consciousness and was about to turn himself into the police? Having been a police officer and seem countless crimes like this up front and personal, I know that nothing in the bad guy's life changed, he got tired, the fun of watching your mother squirm wore off, or he just needed another fix of whatever drug he was on. Nothing in the killer's mind changed, and in my mind, that means he was still a threat to all of us. To you, to me, and if we don't drop him like a hot potato with our 357-magnum, he is still a threat to the greater society.

If we think about Peter's statement, every rule gets in the way of our survival. Police across the country are holding back from responding appropriately to violence. In major cities like Baltimore, Maryland the police aren't even willing to engage criminals due to fear of being arrested or accused of wrongdoing. As a result that crime rates are going through the roof. What will happen to our society if people afraid to shoot a burglar in fear of potential lawsuits, or a man is allowed to stalk your wife for five years, or worse yet, your daughter is murdered by a boyfriend whom she had a restraining order? Every rule gets in the way of our survival, and for now at least, American society is not surviving. The peace, the decency, the social etiquette and the safety of America in the 1950's has intentionally been replaced by lawsuits, unimaginable and grotesque crimes and an entire nation living in fear.

EVERY RULE GETS IN THE WAY OF SURVIVAL.

QUESTIONS ONE SHOULD ASK AFTER A KILLING

1. Did the person killed deserve it, and by what standard?

2. Did the violence perpetrated protect and promote the species? .

3. Did the violence eliminate a dangerous or hostile person or condition in the community?

4. Was the killing justified within the social parameters of accepted norms within the community?

5. Was the killer acting out of belligerence or spite? If so, is this a common occurrence for this individual or family?

6. Is this a random and wanton act?

CHAPTER ELEVEN – UNLOVED CHICKENS

I started off writing this book wanting to explore what I felt was a much-overlooked fact of our lives, that of our species' capacity for aggression and violence was lied about and intentionally distanced by our leading scientists. Growing up, I never felt that social scientists and researchers were ever willing to stand up and take ownership of this natural, primal and basic organism response. I can see where it would be difficult to take even partial responsibility for other members of my own species' deplorable and despicable acts. I know of no sane person who looks at images of the German death camps, or the Cambodian killing fields who isn't sickened by their sight, and morally repelled by the events that took place in them. But that natural repulsion can neither justify nor give the researcher the right to point fingers everywhere except where the fault honestly lay. It is we, the organism, the individual, the family and the society that are responsible for the seeds we sow. Just as the victors of every war place the full blame for the conflict upon the vanquished, it becomes a tired cliché after thousands and millions of innocent people are all killed in these global pissing matches. Trying to make every leader who successfully helped his tribe survive (however briefly) into some anomaly, some uncontrollable and mutated monster all for the sake of deflecting our own collective guilt over how he did it, is ridiculous in the extreme. We can only move forward, honestly move forward as individuals and as families / societies when we accept who and what we are and find workable ways to live with the burden of our biological survival mechanism.

There is not a psychoanalyst in the world who is working with clients in their therapies whose goal is to help the patient learn who they are, what they do, and ultimately to accept themselves…warts and all. But that very same doctor, runs and hides from a patient who is in touch with their natural aggressive self? Aggression is viewed as bad, as sociopath and something to be fixed. Where would the world be today if Alexander the Great, Genghis Khan, Julius Caesar, Captain Cook, Christopher Columbus, George Washington, and President FDR were to have been counseled by doctors to be passive, to avoid their natural aggression and violence? Where would the development of the human race be if these great men's tutors had a zero tolerance for aggression? So ask yourself, why are today's schools, courts, news media and governments around the world trying to so very hard to teach people the New Testament values of "turning the other cheek" and "the meek shall inherit the Earth" when it is just the opposite of who and what we are as people? The only possible reason they are trying to do this is that those in control of those global societies don't want any problems with aggression from individuals. They want to try to breed/ program our species' natural aggression response out of us, so they can control us. They would have us believe that being violent and aggressive is not part of us, is abnormal, is deviant behavior and needs to be strictly controlled. Why would anyone try to lead us away from this simple truth about our human nature? Doing so only serves the rulers who are right this moment trying to pacify the global population.

I've got news for you; the meek shall not inherit the earth. It is the wolves that round up the sheep shall in the night that inherit three hot meals a day. I once read a quote from Benjamin Franklin that read; "A democracy is a sheep and two wolves voting equally on what is for lunch" and unless we all understand that aggression and violence is who and what we are, and that we must return to the world order that comes from that, we will be soon find ourselves subjugated by those who are fully in touch with and allow that aggression and violence. The power-hungry men who forced America to invade Nicaragua in 1915, the men who started World War One, the very same men who convinced Woodrow Wilson that American needed to enter the war, the men who divided up all of Europe, the Middle East, Africa and Asia at the Treaty of Versailles in 1919, the men who started the Jewish boycott of Germany in 1933, the men who started World War Two, are the same men who created all of the rest of the wars and conflicts in the twentieth century. Those same men are still manipulating politicians and the media as I write this and are still voting on what to have for lunch today. And that lunch is you and your family.

If you read history and look at Utopian societies that have existed whose rule of law prohibits the use and display of force and violence, they don't survive for long. Look no further than modern day Tibet. Those monks can pray from sunrise to sunset, and for all their prayers these many years the Chinese military has yet to leave that country. If a peaceful, non-violent society lives within walking distance to a country like ancient Sparta, the peaceful society will be sucking Spartan dick within two weeks. The young men who once were planting crops and singing hymns about God and green grass will be serving as canon fodder in the Sparta Army in short order, and those that aren't dead or sold into slavery will be learning to cook Spartan black broth and fish for their masters. As Mr. Vacco aptly states; "Tyson doesn't care about the chickens" Neither did Hitler, Stalin, or Napoleon or any other ruler in history. And neither should we!

We kill to survive, so that OUR family will survive, that OUR tribe will survive, and that OUR society will survive to see the sun rise one more time. We kill the lame and lazy so that those of us that produce food for our society have the energy to do it again tomorrow. We kill the deadly & the dangerous so that we are not wasting protein energy constantly fighting the same battle over and over again. We kill criminals so that we are not dedicating resources fighting ourselves and not our enemies. We kill the crazy and the demented since they waste resources and produce nothing in return. And as repulsive as the idea of this unbridled lust may seem to modern "civilized" man, you must ask yourself

"What am I willing to do to survive." And if you can't answer that you would kill a grossly deformed child at birth with your own hands, then you and your "Zero Tolerance" schools won't survive America's next clash with a tribe that is willing to do whatever is necessary to survive. Tyson doesn't care about the chickens, why do you? Why do you feel it is all right for your salary to be taxed at 100% to support all of these people?

- o People that don't want to work
- o Can't work due to being deformed or mentally disabled
- o Are incapable of working from birth defects
- o Are too drunk and drugged out to work
- o Too lazy to work
- o Who would rather steal and rob than work

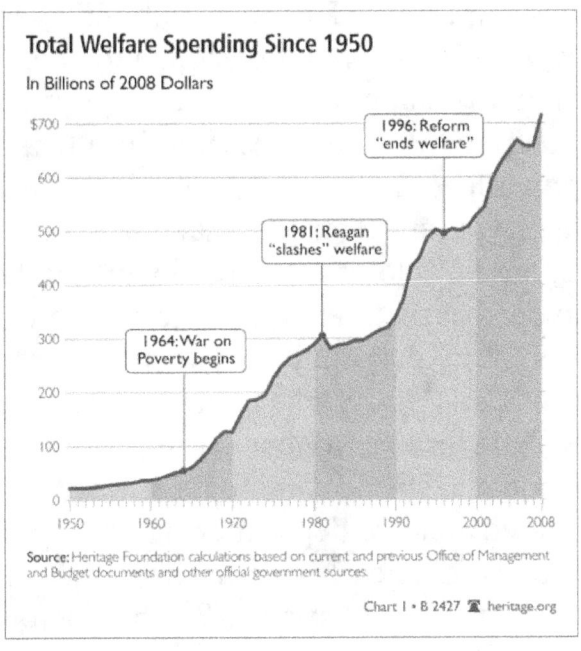

Total Welfare Spending Since 1950

In Billions of 2008 Dollars

1996: Reform "ends welfare"

1981: Reagan "slashes" welfare

1964: War on Poverty begins

Source: Heritage Foundation calculations based on current and previous Office of Management and Budget documents and other official government sources.

Chart 1 • B 2427 ☎ heritage.org

Presidential candidate Mitt Romney was video taped complaining about the 47% of people in the US that don't work. He lost his bid for the White House because of it. But was he wrong in that number? The truth is as of August 16, 2015, that 34.5 percent of the United States is on welfare. Government spending on welfare has increased 700% since President Johnson first declared war on poverty.

Another 15 percent is retired. That leaves 50% of the country working and paying the tax bill for the entire country and the other one hundred and sixty million people who, for various reasons don't want to work.

The ramifications of being in denial about this are played out ever day in your life. Every good and service that you touch is taxed. Every truck that delivers food to the store is taxed, the machinery that is used to process the food and goods you use is taxed. Every item you own has dozens of layers of tax upon it. And then they tax your salary. There is taxation, layer upon layer upon layer of taxation, all designed to keep you and your family running on the wheel in your little fucking cage. Keep running, keep paying for others in society to survive while you sacrifice your self, your family, and your family's future for their sake. How many of our fathers, our kind loving and hard working fathers have to drop dead at the breakfast table before we stop this madness? Why do you think the primary reason American couples divorce is money? It is because society believes everyone is willing to pay 100% of their income to the government for the sake of having roads paved and fire departments at the ready. Our ancestors lived a nearly two million years without fire departments or social services? Why do you believe you can't live without them for forty? With the coming collapse of American society it is time to eliminate the burden and waste of Tier Four Societal Structures on the individual and family.

I began wanting an honest to discuss and form an appraisal of who we are. And after reading through my pages have realized that the first half of this book is nothing more than a primer for this, the second half. Simply elaborating on the problem of who and what we are without giving a working solution and strategy for it, would be a dis-service to the reality of how we as a species survive.

So, the only option I have is to now present a working hypothesis on how best to incorporate these truths into a working formula for our species. I never intended to write a blueprint for a new world order, but I guess that is where this river has lead me. To that end, I must fully confess that I am of the belief that America is in the final stages of its rapid decline into oblivion. Our forefather's dream of Republic where citizens rule their own lives and regal tyranny is quashed by individual freedom and responsibilities was a grand thing when it was written. The Declaration of Independence is an awe-inspiring document. The intent behind it and the Bill of Rights was nothing less than remarkable for its day. But the nation, and the population of the thirteen colonies were a different people then. Our nation's roots at the time were from all from Western Europe and shared a common ancestry, religion, genetics and history. And we are now a much different peoples. That simple government system that Franklin and Jefferson laid out no longer works and is corrupted by special interests, political action corporations, businesses and corporations larger than anything they could have dreamed of. And like ever nation and dream before it, these United States are quickly fading into memory.

I honestly believe that in order for our species to once again find balance as individual organisms and as families, there must be a complete destruction of the societies that now exist. Our global population is far too large, and resource demanding. No organism that is dependent upon so many thousands of other organisms (whose life spans are a fraction of humans) can ever sustain such a massive human population. Our growth in numbers has destroyed the very thing we need to survive, the natural world. We need the honeybee, just as much as the whale. We can have a place in this great and amazing planet, but not in nearly the vast numbers that we now inhabit it. After much thought, I was able to calculate that if all women, now of childbearing age were to only have one child at age thirty we could reduce the global human population from its current 7 billion, down to under 1 billion in about two hundred years. But since there are religions that insist that breeding is a right, not a privilege, they would never agree to it. So we are left with the need for a Zombie Apocalypse to wipe out the entire surplus human species before we can rebuild out of the debris.

And that leads me to this truth, that in the past two hundred years, our population has grown too large. We consume far too many animal and planet resources. And you would have to be a fucking idiot to believe that by the world will be saved from destruction if we just all recycle and love our planet. Please, just fuck me in the head with a spoon. I once worked at an open pit gold mine in eastern Nevada. The hole they had dug in their search for gold was over two miles across and three miles in length. It was eighteen hundred feet below the ground level. Every year, this mine used over three hundred thousand gallons of Cyanide to process the gold out of the paydirt. And on my first day at the mine I was told that there were no Styrofoam cups for coffee because they weren't environmentally friendly. I'm listening to my new boss tell me how bad these cups were for the world, while looking out the window at a hole they dug that was six square miles in diameter and used the equivalent of one hundred tanker truck loads of toxic Cyanide every year of its ten year history. WTF? The reason I bring this up is that everyone is again pointing fingers at things that aren't the problem. The problem is over population of the human species. Not over population of wild Mustangs in Nevada, or too many Blue Fin Tuna in the Pacific, or too many stray cats in Los Angeles. There are just way too many of us, and your using recycled bags at check out time at Trader Joes isn't going to do a god damn thing for the planet or its problems. If you want to really make a fucking dent in all of this. Don't breed. That's it. Just pull out / or turn over / take the morning after pill, or abort the pregnancy. Which, after having just written a hundred pages on the need for our organism to survive sounds pretty funny coming from me.

Another birth control funny is from a recent political protest of Presidential candidate Jeb Bush. The "Black Lives Matter" protesters disrupted Mr. Bush's speaking engagement, and many of the Hispanics who were chanting, "black lives matter" were all seen wearing Planned Parenthood T-shirts. (photo courtesy of Breitbart.com)

According to the Planned Parenthood Corporation, over 2000 African American women have abortions each and every day. That number represents ten percent of that minority's population in the US. And it is a very good start in the overall reduction of our population. But as many have pointed out previously, a Zero Population Growth is nothing more than white genocide. And since 90% of all abortions are performed on white, western women at a time when people of Middle Eastern / Muslim decent represent the largest per capita increase in births in the entire world.

Since it would be nearly impossible to gain enough of a global consensus for massive reductions on the world's populations, we must be content with this section of book to be used post-apocalypse.

The following chapters list guidelines that are based upon the core values presented in this book. As a result, it should be understand when applying them, that the sole rationale behind each of them is for our species to survive long –term with as little societal influence as possible. Also a secondary theme in these suggestions is to allow individuals and families to utilize our biological and natural aggression and violence to our benefit. Combined, I believe we shall return to a balanced life, and one that will reduce the stress we have all been under.

ZOMBIE APOCALYPSE

Chances are, you're already surrounded by mindless, bloodthirsty, half-alive, subhuman wretches. An actual zombie outbreak would just give you an excuse to do something constructive.

CHAPTER TWELVE - SIZE MATTERS

Our intrepid Arctic explorer Peter Vacco has observed in his travels that people in the small villages he hikes through in Canada are much more polite and accommodating. If you ever have had the occasion to go to Kowloon, China, you will have stood in the middle of the most densely populated city in the world. And while in Kowloon you will understand just how Mr. Vacco's observation about Canada is painfully accurate. Thusly the foundation of any new social order must be in limitation of the population size. Several writers have previously suggested various ideal population models for such a working society ranging from a thousand to over twenty thousand persons. After much research, I would recommend a cap at ten thousand inhabitants per community. Anything less than this would not be able to sustain major shifts in environment, hostile neighbors, or community demographic changes. Anything more would require far too great administrative staff to support and would ultimately lead to more or less the same Tier Four Social institutions that we now have. In communities of this size it is relatively easy to maintain lines of communication and responsibility for action, while at the same time allowing individuals the creative freedom necessary to pursing their own paths. By limited the social modules to a specific number, it forces the community to strictly follow procreation guidelines. Remember that by allowing every female to give birth at anytime in they become pregnant, it then demands that a school system is in place at all times to teach off spring. By limiting when and in what year's childbearing females can be issued licenses to become pregnant, it also limits the financial burden on society by limiting the timeframe schools must be in operation.

In addition, by limiting the community size it forces a natural economy and market to develop within each separate community. This in turn allows for and promotes innovation in commerce to address economic and material needs specific to that community. Our post zombie apocalyptic society must be materially and financially self-sufficient as much as is possible to avoid the need of having to create forms of currencies for trade between the various communities. There is really nothing wrong with bartering for goods and services, as our ancestors fully knew this. And more importantly the practice of bartering eliminates the money middlemen, the insurance brokers, the Central Bankers, credit cards, taxation, the moneylenders, and the IRS. In one simple move, you have gotten rid of the majority of the stress in your life, without having to kill a single Internal Revenue Agent. Population control is meant more as a means to reducing the staggering weight that Tier Four Social Structures produce on the individual and family. So they only way to remove this burden is to reduce the number of people, the actual physical infrastructure has to support. In doing so, we can vastly restrict that actual number of people that it takes to administer community business. In addition, by removing the many roles and departments that government is now playing, it will (hopefully) force individuals to start taking care of their own business, their own children, their own safety, their own protection, and their own shit. Irresponsible and incorrigible people in society will quickly learn that they must get up off the couch and start working to make their own living in the world. I should imagine that the first few years of this new social structure will inevitably be a bit of an eye opener for the lame and lazy when the community's capacity for putting up with their shit comes to an abrupt stop. As for the criminally inclined, there will no doubt be a rapid and steep increase in the number of deaths of criminals, followed by a near zero level of burglaries and related mayhem after about the one year anniversary.

Everyone works, everyone contributes…<u>everyone</u>.

CHAPTER THIRTEEN - SPACE

The old saying goes, "Strong fences build good neighbors" and it is important to note that every single study on population density indicates that the closer we (and rats) live to one another, the more stress, aggression and violence is seen in those communities. This body of work is not intended to promote violence, only to acknowledge the primary cause and to develop strategies for dealing with it more effectively so as to not destroy the organism and the world we live in. And by allowing ourselves and our families more room to stretch our legs and live in, we will all have a much lowered need to act out our natural, biological aggression. By all accounts it takes approximately an acre of land to grow 60% of a family's food supply for a year. (variables based on region and climate) Combined with chickens and other small livestock, there should be little other costs incurred by the family to sustain itself. In addition, up to one-eight of the population (one thousand people) should be directly involved with the production of other foods that are meant to supplement the individual family crops, as well as act as a means of commerce with other communities. So we are looking at a land space of approximately twenty-five square miles of any given region. (five by five sq miles) This land size is also small enough of an area to allow an individual to transverse the whole of it in about two hours on foot. This is important in that if we have learned anything by contemporary society, it is that by spending so much time in commuting between work and home, we have replaced quality time with our families with a quantity of time in our cars. This lifestyle further depletes our finances due to the cost of owning, registering, insuring, maintaining, and driving that transportation device. If you spend an hour each way commuting a day, that adds up an average of five hundred hours per year. If you owned a one acre plot of your own and produced food on it, after the initial planting of the crops, you could conceivably spend as little as five hundred hours a year working on the crops, and never have to go back into the cubes ever again. You are undoubtedly seeing a trend here. As much as I personally love first person shooter games on X-box something has got to give in our contemporary lifestyles. I see that much of my time is being spent on just making enough money to stay afloat and trying to stay ahead of or catching up with the IRS. We work and work and work and work, and commute and commute and when we wake up the next morning, we haven't made any progress in getting to a point we can just breathe. Getting all of us back to basics doesn't mean we have to all become Amish and return to buttons and kerosene lamps. But there certainly needs to be more of a relationship between our work and our families. What good is it for both parents to work their butts off 14 hours a day for their families and then only spend an hour running in circles around the kids at night? I've seen this time and again. The parents come home exhausted, tired and frustrated from the boss and long drive home. Your kids Fascist teachers are have spent the last six hours indoctrinating your kids and now that they are home and off the leash they are acting out. The parents run around the house barking more orders at the kids until they all go into their respective rooms to surrender to another day. The parents spend a few moments with their window open smoking pot and the kids are texting their friends complaining about what dicks their parents are and how they can't wait to leave home. Am I far off here? There are millions of versions of this scenario being played out every single day. But this is not a home, this is not a family and it sure as hell is not what The Prime Directive of our species requires of us to raise off spring. With this scene played out in most American families every day, is it no wonder that Dylan Klebold's parents didn't know their kid was sawing off shotgun barrels and making bombs in his room, not ten feet from the family kitchen?

FUCK ME!

This sorry ass excuse for child rearing isn't really Dylan's parent's fault. Sure, there are parents that are able to spend more time and attention on their kids. But they can only do so as a result of having greater finances available to them. The issue is not trying to catch up with the Joneses to be able to spend more quality time with your kids. The issue is changing the Tier Four Social Structure around so greatly that the family is a functional unit once more that is in a position to do its job more effectively. We can do this only by reducing our dependence upon consumer goods and basic food purchases. We also need to send our governments home and start over from scratch so that they support families rather than strip families of all their income and responsibility.

In order for that to happen, people need space for kids to run amuck around the house, and for parents and kids to grow the majority of their own food. This can only be done when every family has more space to live in, unhindered by other families and society.

The "new" family structure is based upon the individual being fully responsible for their survival. Those of you who don't want to give up your second and third homes in resort communities, or your high end luxury cars, will have to learn to adjust your lifestyle accordingly. Earning money, while creating nothing of value must (and will shortly) end. The creation of wealth without the creation of goods and production is meaningless and ultimately will destroy the economy and society that allows that to happen. Earning money through charging interest to others is just as damaging. I am certain Carl Marx said it much better than I could ever.

Your trophy wives will have to learn to live without spending long hours in the salon, and day spa. She will no longer be the princess and have to clean her own home, her own dishes, and raise her own children. Having a segment of any society that lives like this is an insult and affront to our entire species.

CHAPTER FOURTEEN – FAMILY

So, here is where the fun starts; in attempting to plan out a new world order. Remembering the Vaccoism: Every rule you *have to obey*, and makes you weaker and limits the ability to respond to new situations. (or something like that)

The only thing I would add here is that this is where it all happens. And in order for individuals to grow up right/good/properly/not crazy, we need families that are more, (than less) functional during this lengthy process, and who support the children's journey. Now, not everyone is going to produce off spring and that is all right. We don't need to force the population into breeding. But what is important is that there is a family structure in place to support all members of the clan. Even if an older brother is turning forty and hasn't met that right woman yet, or is perhaps gay, he and his parents and other siblings need to stay together to support one another as a family. We all need to move back home. We need to go get our parents out of the nursing home and bring them back into the family fold. We need to stop paying for child support and have our parents watch our kids while we are working. We need families again.

It wasn't always like this in America. We had families once. But then World War Two broke out and millions of our young men went to fight. When those men came home from the war, the government needed to compensate them for their efforts and the government offered returning soldiers two options. The US offered either free college, or a no interest loan on a new home. And millions of those men picked a new home. Part of this was from the fact that they went to war as boys, but came of age in the war. By the time they came back, they all had one thing on their minds...The Prime Directive. So they picked the home, rather than education. This was the single most destructive thing that had ever happened to American family structure in our entire history and within a few short years parents and their children and their grandchildren no longer lived in the same house or city. Siblings, instead of living just down the hall and under the same roof, lived in different cities. Adult children now lived in the suburbs and then they needed a car for each adult parent to get around the vast distances of suburbia. Our commute times increased exponentially to the distance from the business centers that remained in the heart of the downtown sections. The children then had to be watched not by the grandparents, but by paid baby sitters, which in turn decreased disposal income, which in turn increased the burden on the working parents to generate more money. These large suburbs demanded more physical infrastructure to support sewer, power, water and roads and again demanded more taxes from the family. And when that first suburban generation of children grew up, it was they who in the late 1960's rebelled against authority in mass. It was they who protested the Vietnam War in mass, it was they who initiated the "Summer of Love" and became beatniks and hippies. It was they who would come out of the closet in gay communities around the country. And the world as we knew it changed all because the War took our nation's children and gave us back millions of battle weary veterans, no-interest home loans.

CHAPTER FIFTEEN – COMMUNITY AFFAIRS

Nearly every society throughout history eventually codifies a series of rules based on core values that are shared within the community whose sole purpose is to settle differences between its members. It will always happen! When enough people in the community get sick and tired of a particular issue, they band together, demand redress and insist that everyone in the group get in line or fucking leave. It is bound to happen to every group of people. There will always be a select group of folks that just keep making other people's lives fucking miserable and eventually, collectively people lay down what is loosely termed "The Law" just so they can sleep at night without the jerk next door killing another wife, or neighbor, or stranger and causing a stink. For hundreds of years Germany's Visigoths were a nomadic peoples that moved about that section of current day Europe being raiders, looting, killing, and taking what they wanted. Eventually after the cool down period of the 500's CE, they began settling down in and around Germany and were forced with a new conundrum. They soon discovered that they needed laws to deal with things that previously would be dealt with mano-e-mano, and wrote a series of rules for folks to live by, that today are called the Visigoth Code of Laws of 650 CE.

Page 216 Visigoth Code of Laws. ANCIENT LAW.

VIII. Where One Freeborn Person Strikes Another.

If one freeborn person should inflict a wound upon another, and the wounded person should die at once, the attacking party shall be punished for homicide; and if he who was wounded should not die immediately, the aggressor must either be confined in prison, or released on bail. Should the person who was wounded escape with his life, he who injured him must pay him twenty solidi, on account of the attack alone; and, if he should not have that sum, he shall receive two hundred lashes in public, and, in addition to this, he shall be compelled to pay such damages, for the wound he inflicted, as may be assessed by the judges.

This fifteen hundred year old manuscript is not much different from the current California State Penal Code. *CALIFORNIA PENAL CODE SECTION 505. Justifiable Homicide: Self-Defense or Defense of Another*

The defendant is not guilty of (murder/ [or] manslaughter/ attempted murder/ [or] attempted voluntary manslaughter) if (he/ she) was justified in (killing/attempting to kill) someone in (self-defense/ [or] defense of another). The defendant acted in lawful (self-defense/ [or] defense of another) if:

> 1. The defendant reasonably believed that (he/she/ [or] someone else/ [or] *<insert name or description of third party>*) was in imminent danger of being killed or suffering great bodily injury [or was in imminent danger of being (raped/maimed/robbed/ *<insert other forcible and atrocious crime>*)];

2. The defendant reasonably believed that the
immediate use of deadly force was necessary
to defend against that danger;

All peoples, dating back to the very beginning of time
have laid down the law when things became too rowdy,
too uncontrollable or just too extreme. But I really
believe that before we start "laying down the law" in
our post zombie apocalypse we need to go back to our
two basic premises, "Every law weakens our ability to
respond to changing situations" And # 2, Is the
situation or behavior as it stands…sustainable?"
I think that referring back to these simple parameters
will allow the community to quickly find a balance
between writing and enforcing more rules, and whether
or not a rule even needs to be introduced…as yet.
Because every rule you make will eventually require
someone to enforce it, and yes, unless the entire section
of a town that a party is being thrown in is willing to
get up out of bed, and go knock on the person that is
making the noise; then the community will naturally
gravitate toward hiring agents to enforce rules. Then
judges are needed, and juries, and prisons and on and
on again. This in turn will lead to more demand by the
system for more money and resources from families.
You just can't get away from it…fuck!
    I bring this example up at the beginning of this
chapter first, rather as an addendum to it, because our
new society needs to have a system of community
governing that is by default: _**lean and mean**_. I
recommend never any more than one or two hundred
persons working in the function of community
governing in any ten thousand-person community. And

these roles are strictly regulators and investigators. They observe and report. It then becomes the responsibility of individuals within the community to take action. NOT THE GOVERNMENT! In our, and thousands of other communities in the past the issue of taxation upon goods has been the singular most burdensome of all issues. And in order to avoid this burden, I can determine no other means that by replacing it than with a community labor requirement, This brings up a tricky wicket.

SLAVERY.

In days gone by all societies have allowed for the taking and holding of slaves. Slavery is more than just a means of punishing the vanquished of a battle. In order to feed the slaves, they would inevitably be put to use in the production of food for the family, or community. Those very same slaves built nearly every community building in the ancient world, from the Egyptian Pyramids to the Roman Coliseum and the Great Wall of China. Until quite recently, stronger peoples have always ruled weaker peoples. To this very day, slavery exists everywhere in the world, including the United States. The practice consists of going into poor, weak countries and enticing, lying, or capturing the locals and forcing them to do the work that you want them to do is nothing new. Today's corporate high-tech slave brought into the United States from India to work for pennies is no less a type of slave to his circumstance, than any other slave in history. Slavery allows the members of a community to expand the production of goods, services and food far beyond the limits of the physical capacity of that community. Much has been written about the ill effects upon the lives of people who have been forced into slavery. There is so much hyperbole about the American Civil War these days, that we forget that the people who are now protesting about the Confederate Flag and how bad slavery was, were the weaker peoples that were turned into slavery because of their weakness.

This brings us to another Vaccoism. "Don't lose."

When you are in conflict with another society, make certain that you, your leaders, your military, and your society is in the game 100%. Get your head in the game and keep it there until you win. Don't settle for anything less than winning. Wars and conflicts in the new (and old) world are not liberal kindergartens where everyone gets a medal for participating. Fuck no! Conflicts are about land, property, resources, water, or elimination of threats. If you don't want to be tracked down and killed for your participation in a war that you lost, sixty years after the fact, then *don't lose!* Losing is a sure-fire way to being made into a slave.

Slaves suck Spartan dick…DON'T LOSE. Tis better to die in the effort then lose and be forced to live as a slave with your shame.

Back to the task at hand…defining a government. It is vital for the health and happiness of individuals and families moving forward beyond the Post Zombie Apocalypse that a lot of thought be put into defining what "GOVERNMENT" means and what that social entity's role in the community should be, and more importantly where the boundaries of human and societal responsibility are drawn. I would at all times during this process of definition, fall back to a solid, old time stand by expression: KEEP IT SIMPLE STUPID. If followed, I don't believe that any fledgling start up community could be held at fault for initial failings. By not depending upon Tier Four Social Structures for our daily bread, it makes our children stronger, more independent, and more capable of adapting to the changes that naturally occur in the world and in our lives.

Friends I know who work as firefighters in Nevada were asked to travel to Louisiana immediately after Hurricane Katrina to render aid. They said that about two hundred miles outside of New Orleans, the people they encountered in rural Louisiana survived the event with little inconvenience. Many lived outside as their homes were damaged beyond usability. But those people were doing pretty well in spite of it all. As the firefighters traveled closer and closer to the New Orleans metropolitan area, the people they encountered became more and more desperate and were having tremendous difficulty dealing with the situation. The only real difference my friends could tell was not the physical challenge of the aftermath of the hurricane, but the inner city residents had a long history on the aid and comfort of the government, rather than the rural residents who were much more independent of government intervention and dependence during normal times. I bring this up only to point out, that the more DEPENDENT we are upon society, the less likely we are to cope adequately during stress times. The natural world is not stable, it is not controllable, and as a result our organism must always be able to stand on its own two feet, and make it across the river better than any Wildebeest ever could. Eliminating our current dependency upon Tier Four Social Structures, and they ultimate destruction of them should be our top priority as a species. Rebuilding after the post Zombie Apocalypse will require our communities to maintain only a bare minimum of annually retentive bean counters purely for the sake of command and control, rather than rulers and kings.

Further I would highly recommend that communities look to diversify the spectrum of goods and services that it produces. Dependence upon one industry for the entire community will have significantly higher risks for the long term prospects of that community than one whose labor, manufacturing, agriculture and production can not suffer from one death blow like happened to the once great city of Detroit, Michigan. It had one industry and when the North American Free Trade Agreement went into affect, the city went from nearly three million down to six hundred thousand. The auto manufacturing collapse left behind only the poor and illiterate and there has not been property tax coming into the city in over twenty years. It's important to think things through as a community. Look to the past and figure out if you're about to walk the way of the Romans, or the slaves. Talk to your neighbors, talk to the movers and shakers in your new community. Figure out how best to reduce the overall risk to commerce and food production until things can stabilize.

Further, the only way a community like this is going to ever survive without creating a new super class of every expanding government agencies is for everyone to commit to about five hours of volunteer time each week. Every man, woman, and child must pitch in on community projects. I would suggest everyone puts Friday morning aside to help build the community. This time could also be well used in the training of martial arts and military practice. There is nothing like clearing a road for three hours and then target practice to work out some teenage angst. This all borders on socialism, but when all of this great country lie in ashes from the Zombie Apocalypse, keeping people's bodies engaged and focused on re-enforcing the walls against the next Zombie attack, will keep their minds from dwelling on their hunger.

CHAPTER SIXTEEN – KILL ALL LAWYERS

In William Shakespeare's play Henry the Sixth, the famous words, "The first thing we do is to kill all lawyers" And not that I wish any particular lawyer dead, but once again, lawyers in Tier Four Social Structures represent the extreme distance that people now have from The Prime Directive. We no longer have a voice in our own lives, as we must stifle them and turn our rage, our grievances, and our insult over to the millions of lawyers and courts that have set up shop for the sake of stealing our freedoms and responsibilities. Insults are now met with court dates, injuries are met with litigation, and murder is met with book, line and verse rather than swift and undeniable justice. Nothing hinders future murders by the lame and lazy quite like immediate and hard retribution / justice handed out by the family of the victims. I was in India a few years back when I saw a large crowd of people chasing and eventually capturing an older man accused of molesting a six-year-old girl in the neighborhood. He was immediately pounced upon by the crowd and kicked to death in a matter of seconds. Given the dreadful state of the Indian infrastructure and government, the police showed up only after the man's blood had dried on the roadway where he was left dead for his untried crime. It mattered not if he was guilty; the accusation alone was enough of an indictment for his murder. This kind of street justice is common throughout the world, except in the "civilized" Western world. Vigilantism is viewed as the worse kind of individual action by a society that wishes to control every act and deed through its intermediaries… the police, lawyers, judges, and juries.

In our new family society, it is vital to eliminate the bureaucratic middle men that now fill the ranks of government offices and prohibit, (have a zero tolerance for) people taking the law into their own hands. Personal responsibility for one's own safety must be the number one rule of thumb that people live by. After this society collapses from the unhindered greed and reign of terror that parasitic demigods that now run it have caused, it will be equally important to ensure that these subspecies of society are not allowed to take root in the new community. And to that end it is critical that we kill off any of the vestiges of the old social order before we can move into the next paradigm. To do that, I present the following as a partial list of those people/roles that need to fade along with the old flags of the United States.

- o POLITICIANS
- o POLITICAL ADVISORS
- o LAWYERS
- o SUPREME COURTS
- o CENTRAL BANKS AND CENTRAL BANKERS
- o BANKS, MONEY LEANDERS, LOAN SHARKS
- o COMODITY BROAKERS, STOCK TRADERS
- o LAW ENFORCEMENT AUTHROTIES
- o HOSPITALS & NURSING HOMES

- o TRAFFIC COPS
- o BUILDING INSPECTORS
- o HEALTH INSPECTORS
- o SCHOOL TEACHERS AND ADMINISTRATORS
- o ANYTHING TO DO WITH HIGHER EDUCATION
- o REPORTERS, JOURNALISTS, BLOGGERS,
- o ART SCHOOLS
- o ANIMAL CONTROL
- o RESTAURANTS & HOTELS
- o MANUFACTURING THAT REQUIRES WATER FOR PROCESS
- o CAR MANUFACTURERS
- o HELLO KITTY PRODUCTS
- o EVERYTHING MADE IN CHINA
- o AID TO FOREIGN COUNTRIES
- o SOCIAL WELFARE
- o FOOD STAMPS, SECTION EIGHT HOUSING,
- o AA MEETINGS
- o DID I MENTION HELLO KITTY CRAP?

When one attempts to, "Keep It Simple Stupid," it becomes necessary to cut away all of the fat from our lives. This can only be done by the total elimination of Tier Four Society Structures and then after seeing what works (given the current situations) and what doesn't that we slowly add only those society elements that serve the community at the time, and only while remembering the horrific burden that these institutions ultimately imposed upon the individual and the family. I am certain that were be people that will not want, or be prepared to take on the full responsibility for their lives after the Shit Hits The Fan. But that day is fast approaching, and the sooner you get use to dealing with your own problems the more likely it is that you and your family will survive the Zombie Apocalypse.

CHAPTER SEVENTEEN – YOU KILL ME

With the coming destruction of Tier Four Societies a lot of things will get very simple for you. No more speeding tickets, no more IRS and taxes, no presidential primaries, and no more social infrastructure. And all this is good for the soul. But you will quickly learn that you are now 100% responsible for your own actions, and your own safety. If you had a tendency to be an asshole while driving or making a lot of noise around your neighbors late at night in the past, maybe played the role of benevolent belligerent boss, you would do well to not practice those behaviors in the new world. Being an asshole (for the foreseeable future) will most likely get your legs broken at the very least, or a bullet through the head depending upon the temperament of the next person you piss off. And all those other highly irritating things you do around people, might even offer the opportunity to one of your old friends, an excuse to kick the living shit out of you…for good measure and old time's sake.

After the collapse, the crème de la crème of our society will very quickly rise to the top of the food chain, and start making his own rules for your little community. Assholes and the lame and lazy must be prepared to either put up and quickly get in line with the big dog, or to challenge him and maybe even…possibly take over the clan yourself. There will be no middle ground in the future. Sheep or wolves, you have to make up your mind right now which side of this fence you want to live on. If you decide that a particular community is just far too violent for your tastes, you can always move to the lovely town of Mayberry. It might give you a momentary reprieve from the hostility and aggression of the first clan, but eventually every community is going to be fighting off other communities for resources and materials. It will be Alexander the Great, Genghis Khan, the Visigoths, the Vikings and Hitler all over again. And it's not going to be all killing, all the time. That is just not sustainable. Your clan will quickly develop rules that unless another clan member is a prick that has done real harm to you, or is some how trying to fuck you over; you won't be able to just go about your clan killing at will. Even the occasional outburst and killing spree on your clan's enemies won't always be tolerated. The other community might just make the metal that your community must have to make farm equipment. The best rule of thumb for jerks in the new world is to not shit in your own nest.

So I am warning you, that you have two choices.

1. Stop being an asshole right now and start working effectively with your neighbors.
2. Or go buy some bananas and start practicing for sucking Spartan dick.

Your life just got very simple. The choices you can make at any given time just got extremely fucking simple. If you want to survive, and want your kids to survive you have got to get your balls to drop after decades of them being kicked up inside of you. Or be ready to learn to suck your more aggressive neighbor's dick. Once society breaks down, or breaks away from Tier Four structures, it all falls right back on you and your family to survive. So! Survive and get your ass in gear. Get in touch with your inner primal self. (I just love writing that touchy feely shit on paper) GET IN TOUCH WITH YOUR INNER SELF. Don't believe all of the hype that you have evolved and are just too limp wrested to get butch. Truth is, no one is beyond being capable of grotesquely horrific violence. NO ONE!

The trick to it is by ALWAYS PUTTING YOUR OWN SELF, YOUR OWN FAMILY, AND YOUR OWN CLAN SURVIVAL FIRST. This needs to be your only rule of thumb. Why do you think we have gotten away from this to begin with? By promoting generosity and loving your neighbors, and giving to those needy souls in other countries it weakens us. It puts other tribes before our own. It weakens us financially, morally, and militarily. But going into wars, winning, and then walking away without any financial benefits from that war (loot, slaves, oil, gold etc) it weakens us. The people who made their money ten fold on every war the USA has entered, were the bankers and military equipment producers who lent the money for war material production.

Why do you think our government left behind all those nifty jeeps, and trucks, and planes in Europe after World War Two? Or in Vietnam and Afghanistan after those conflicts? We were told that it was too costly to pay to return them. No, it was the bankers and military establishments way of ensuring that the government didn't reuse and resell that surplus to recoup some of the cost of production. It was their way to ensure that our taxes will be used to buy new equipment and jeeps and trucks and planes. The American family has been taxed for a century by the burden of winning without the benefits of conquest.

Everything else is inconsequential and every thing else is bullshit. Kill who you have to, kill if you're afraid, kill without caring and kill without looking back. Your tribe, our tribes, our families, and our country is ALL THAT MATTERS. After you help the first couple of assholes to see the error of their ways, you won't even know you've killed a person.

Kill who you have to, kill if you're afraid, kill without caring and kill without looking back.

As inspiration to you, and to show you how easy it is to kill, I have inserted this gallery of serial killers who can serve as your inspiration for the Post Zombie Apocalypse. There are so many different ones to pick from that I just didn't have room to put them all.

Now, I am not suggestion that you run out and just start whacking people. I am putting this in the book as a reminder that we all need to be ready to deal with other's violence and aggression right now! There are no more options for putting the responsibility for our clan's, family and personal safety onto any one else. Those days are gone, welcome to the world that your great-great-great grandfather lived in. What will eventually happen is what has always happened when structured societies collapse. After an initial but painful period of raunchy blood filled streets of killings, things settle down in the community to a dull roar, and people once again learn to work collaboratively. But without the overwhelming amount of bullshit and assaults and rapes and robberies that we are living with presently. People are much more polite when there are fewer of us, and the ones that are alive are all armed and in touch with their aggressive survival mode.

CHAPTER EIGHTEEN - CONCLUSION

What started out a few years ago as a book about the selfishness of humans, has evolved into something else. The more I contemplated my own species the harder it was for me to ignore the most basic truth about us. Like many others, I had grown up a firm believer in Darwinism. I took his words and held them against the light of what I saw myself to be, and it was good. Our tools were my accomplishments, our moonwalk, my proof that we were no longer animals living in the jungle.
We had evolved as a species, I told myself. We were no longer beasts of burden, beasts living violent lives in the wilderness.

Our music, our painting and sculptures, our fine china and cathedrals were solid, irrefutable proof that Darwin was right and we were no longer like apes, living in trees throwing feces at one-another. And were it not for the daily grind of news about wars, killings and mayhem, I might have continued permanently to believe in that lie.

I still want to believe in it.

But only fools lie to themselves. So here we are, facing ourselves in the mirror, naked and ashamed. For no righteous person can look at the world that our species has created and not feel a sense of total shame. Against all logic our violent world challenges us to question our false belief that we .... have evolved. The only thing that matters is what we are going to do with this newfound recognition of our violent self.

Its who we are and what we do, that must be accepted and then built upon. Through this work, I have urge you to take back your life from the masters who now rule, or are trying to rule us. I urge you to take back your own responsibility for yourself and your family. I urge you to forget the lies and propaganda that those who want to rule you have integrated into our society, our politics, and our media.

In order for your children and grandchildren to grow up free human beings, you must break away from the concept that we live in civil, social societies, and get back to basics. We are animals, fighting for our own and our children's survival. We are either in an alpha male dominated tribe that is free and subjugates the other tribes we come into contact with. Or we are the subjugated slaves and servants to the more aggressive alpha tribes.

There are no warmNfuzzy, metrosexual male, women are equal, guns are bad, bullying is not nice, can't we all just get along tribes. This utopian ideal is pure propaganda pushed by those who control and manipulate the media. It is put forth to manipulate public discourse so that it is easier for them to subjugate us. They do this by funding hundreds of "grass roots" organizations which promote that warmNfuzzy agenda. The first name that comes to mind is that of George Soros. Each year he gives nearly a half billion dollars to organizations across the globe whose sole purpose is to destabilize legitimate and sovereign governments. Please go out and look at the governments that he has, and continues to try to destabilize. They are all alpha led governments. Yet Soros is only one of dozens of individuals around the world that is working against you, and against your family.

You and your family and communities are being held hostage by these sociopaths, psychopaths and murderous thugs that work day and night to try to control the world. Here in the United States, our elected officials don't care

about our families. They don't care about how their Senate
and House bills affect the people and the families of this
nation. They only care about how their financial backers
think about their work. They only care about their own
personal power and wealth. In spite of our Founding
Father's greatest intention to not set up yet another
kingdom and royal court in the United States, they did just
that by not limiting the number of years of civil service for
our Congressmen and Senators to just six years in the
Constitution. These power brokers are hard at work,
finding new and creative ways to strip you and me of our
personal power. They do this by taxing our families so
greatly that they collapse under the weight. They do this by
giving and supporting other people and families that are
too lazy and too dysfunctional to live without aid. They do
this by thousands of social programs that puts the burden
on you, the functional mother and father to support those
that are not contributing members of our tribe. They do it
by ignoring inter-tribal tensions, they do it by the burden
of taxation on everything we touch or taste. They do it be
suggesting that violence in the name of self-defense is no
longer necessary. They do it by promoting the concept that
calling 911 is the answer to all social problems. They do it
by restrictive gun laws. They do it by holding their police
back from enforcing the law when it comes to certain
minority groups within our tribe. They do it by lifting up
and promoting and sanctioning abnormal behavior from
members of our society.

Some say that for the sake of living in community, that
we must give up *some* personal freedom. My response is
simple. If we are to live in communities, then that
community must share my values. The people in my
community must share full responsibility for the growth,

wellbeing and survival of every member of their family and for this community.

The days when 35% of society is supported by the other 65% must end. The days when 15% of society is not expected to follow the laws that the other 85% follow... must end. We are now at a cross road in this country. We have half of America believing in our sovereignty, and half of it wanting open borders. This is an untenable situation. This proves that the masters of the universe, like Soros, has already won over half of our nation with their propaganda. It proves beyond a shadow of a doubt to me that this nation will not last much long.

And until that day comes, I urge each of you to embrace your true self. Embrace your natural aggressiveness, your natural defensiveness of your family and children. Defend your life, defend your family, defend your tribe. Let all the warmNfuzzys suck Spartan dick. I for one, never acquired the taste for it.

One day you will know that it is time to: "Cry Havoc and let slip the dogs of war"

When that day comes, allow yourself to fully release that primal drive to survive out in the open. Be angry, be enraged, be aggressive and be violent, fight for your right to be your own man, to raise your own family with the values you know to be right and true. Stand up and fight for the right to be the man, the woman, the family and the clan that you truly are.

Biology *is* destiny.

THE END

www.ingramcontent.com/pod-product-compliance
Lightning Source LLC
Chambersburg PA
CBHW071356280526
45787CB00001B/345